DATE DUE

HONG KONG

Falaq Kagda & Magdalene Koh

 **Marshall Cavendish**
Benchmark

New York

PICTURE CREDITS

Cover photo: © E & E Image Library/HIP/The Image Works

alt.TYPE / Reuters: 45 • Chris Davis: 7, 15, 18, 23, 31, 41, 87, 103, 115, 116, 117, 119, 120, 124, 127 • Corbis Inc.: 79, 128 • David Simson: 13, 81, 86, 110 • Focus Tem, Italy: 12, 62, 76, 94, 95, 96 • Getty Images: 89, 99 • Giulio Andreini Photography: 74, 92, 112 • Graham Uden: 33, 98 • HBL Network Photo Agency: 5, 25, 30, 38, 40, 42, 72, 100, 101, 111, 118 • Holzbachovoa/Benet: 56, 77 • Hulton Getty: 19, 20, 21, 22 • Hutchison Library: 24, 28, 97, 123 • International Photobank: 3, 11, 17, 55, 126 • Lonely Planet Images: 16, 43, 48, 49, 50, 53, 54, 66, 76, 82, 90, 109, 121 • Mark Graham: 15, 32, 57, 69 • MCIA—Thomas Khoo: 130 • National Geographic Image Collection: 1, 6, 26, 27, 34, 35, 60, 64, 65, 114, 122 • Nik Wheeler: 9, 37, 39, 59, 62, 63, 71, 84, 105, 106, 107 • Photolibrary.com: 44, 52, 108, 131 • Pietro Scozzari: 102 • Robert Pateman: 61 • Topham Picture Point: 4, 8, 125 • Travel Ink Ltd.: 29, 36, 67, 70, 75, 80, 83, 93, 104

PRECEDING PAGE

Hong Kong ladies in their traditional costume.

Editorial Director (U.S.): Michelle Bisson
Editors: Deborah Grahame, Mabelle Yeo, Mindy Pang
Copyreader: Tara Koellhoffer
Designer: Bernard Go Kwang Meng
Cover picture researcher: Connie Gardner
Picture researcher: Thomas Khoo

Marshall Cavendish Benchmark
99 White Plains Road
Tarrytown, NY 10591
Web site: www.marshallcavendish.us

Library of Congress Cataloging-in-Publication Data
Kagda, Falaq.
  Hong Kong / by Falaq Kagda & Magdalene Koh.—2nd ed.
    p. cm.—(Cultures of the world)
  Summary: "Provides comprehensive information on the geography, history,
    wildlife, governmental structure, economy, cultural diversity, peoples,
    religion, and culture of Hong Kong"—Provided by publisher.
  Includes bibliographical references and index.
  ISBN 978-0-7614-3034-6
  1. Hong Kong (China)—Juvenile literature. I. Koh, Magdalene. II. Title.

DS796.H74K34 2009
951.25—dc22   2007048285

Printed in China

9 8 7 6 5 4 3 2 1

CONTENTS

Although the number of people living on boats is dwindling, the sea still plays an important part in Hong Kong's economy and culture.

A colorful pagoda located within the Temple of Ten Thousand Buddhas.

INTRODUCTION

MENTION "HONG KONG" and images of skyscrapers come to mind. This bustling metropolis has come a long way from its humble beginnings as a fishing village. Today the territory is one of the most crowded cities in the world. Office blocks and apartments jostle for space as streets pulsate constantly with life. But step out of the urban jungle and Hong Kong's serene personality emerges.

Hong Kong's transition from a British colony to China's Special Administrative Region has been eventful. The historic handover on July 1, 1997, evoked mixed feelings. Although initial fears have not materialized, worries over the people's lack of political rights continue to linger.

A decade after the transition Hong Kong has prospered as the gateway to China. It has emerged relatively unscathed after surviving a rash of global pandemics and regional financial meltdowns. Once again Hong Kong's much-feted economy is slowly becoming healthy.

GEOGRAPHY

HONG KONG IS A TERRITORY of China, situated on its southeastern coast. It is made up of a section of the mainland and 235 islands of various sizes, with a total land area of 422 square miles (1,092 square km)—about six times the size of Washington, D.C.

To the north the Sham Chun River forms Hong Kong's border with the rest of China. The Chinese city of Guangzhou (Canton) is around 60 miles (100 km) away, at the mouth of the Zhu Jiang (Pearl) River. Hong Kong is partially situated in the delta of this river. The territory's other close neighbor is Macao, a Portuguese colony, which is located on the opposite side of the Zhu Jiang River delta.

Although Hong Kong has no states or provinces, it can be divided into three main regions based on the territory's geography and history. Hong Kong Island was the site of the original settlement. It remains the administrative and economic center. Including its nearby islets, this region covers 35 square miles (90 square km). The Kowloon Peninsula on the mainland and Stonecutters Island, which were the next areas to become part of the territory, cover 10 square miles (26 square km). The New Territories, made up of a large area on the mainland, Lantau Island, and many smaller islands, have a combined area of 377 square miles (976 square km).

Much of Hong Kong is hilly, and a significant amount of the low-lying terrain is made up of land that has been reclaimed from the sea. Only about 12 percent of the land is forested, but small tropical and subtropical plants are abundant elsewhere. Hong Kong's small amount of fertile soil is concentrated in the mainland portion of the New Territories, near Deep Bay.

Above: **A peaceful scene along the rocky coastline of Hong Kong Island located at Shek O.**

Opposite: **Twilight view of a bay lying along the southern shore of Hong Kong Island.**

PHYSICAL FEATURES

MOUNTAINS Hong Kong is part of a partially submerged mountain range. A series of ridges runs from northeast to southwest, with the highest mountain, Tai Mo Shan, rising to 3,140 feet (957 m). Other mountains include Lantau Peak (3,064 feet/934 m) and Sunset Peak (2,851 feet/869 m) on Lantau Island, Kowloon Peak (1,978 feet/603 m) on the peninsula, and Victoria Peak (1,818 feet/554 m) and Mount Parker (1,739 feet/531 m) on Hong Kong Island. Many of the mountains are composed of volcanic rocks. On the islands the steep slopes drop down abruptly to the sea. Some of the small islands are little more than uninhabited, sea-swept rocks.

RIVERS The only river of any size in Hong Kong is the Sham Chun River in the north, which forms the border with mainland China. It flows into Deep Bay after collecting a number of small tributaries. Elsewhere in Hong Kong small streams flow down the sides of the mountain ridges. Reservoirs and catchment systems have reduced the amount of water that is available downstream.

LOWLANDS Floodplains, river valleys, and reclaimed land occupy less than 20 percent of the land in Hong Kong. The largest lowland areas are in the New Territories, north of Tai Mo Shan. This is where most of Hong Kong's farming is done. The main urban areas—the Kowloon Peninsula and coast of Hong Kong Island—take up only around 10 percent of the level land. Land is constantly being reclaimed from the sea. The scarcity of level land has led Hong Kong's real estate prices, especially in the urban areas, to soar to among the highest in the world.

The agricultural land of the New Territories is divided into thousands of tiny farms.

VICTORIA HARBOR Hong Kong's spectacular deepwater harbor was the major reason that the British chose the site as their trading base in the 19th century. The harbor is well protected by the mountains on Hong Kong Island. Hong Kong's administrative center, usually known simply as the Central District, lies on the northwest coast of Hong Kong Island. The city of Kowloon lies on the other side of the harbor.

CLIMATE

Hong Kong lies just south of the Tropic of Cancer and has a subtropical climate. Its seasonal changes are well marked with hot, humid summers and cool, dry winters. Daily temperature averages range from 59°F (15°C) in February to 87°F (31°C) in July.

Hong Kong's warm subtropical climate provides perfect weather for swimming and relaxing on the beach.

During the summer Hong Kong is buffeted by the monsoon—a moist, warm equatorial wind built up by pressure systems over the Pacific Ocean. The monsoon brings heavy rainfall between May and August, resulting in floods and mudslides. Typhoons are abundant in summer.

In the winter months pressure builds up over Inner Mongolia, bringing dry, colder winds from the landmass in the west. The dry weather causes water shortages in the cities, forcing Hong Kong to import water from mainland China. Currently the region imports over 80 percent of its potable, or drinkable, water from southern China's Guangdong Province.

An average of 85 inches (2.16 m) of rain falls in Hong Kong each year. More than half of this falls during the summer months between May and

September. Only about 10 percent of yearly rain falls from November to March.

FLORA

Many tropical and temperate species of flora are found in Hong Kong. Most of the land area is covered with leafy tropical plants, including mangrove and other swamp plants. The Hong Kong Herbarium, founded in 1878, has about 35,000 specimens, including almost 2,000 known indigenous species and varieties.

After centuries of cutting, burning, and exposure, only 12 percent of Hong Kong's land remains forested. The most common trees are pines, such as the native South China red pine and the slash pine, introduced from Australia. Most of Hong Kong's forest cover, which includes eucalyptus, banyan, casuarina, and palm trees, is the result of reforestation programs started since World War II. Forestry plantations within water catchment areas, country parks, and special areas are managed by the Agriculture and Fisheries Department. Fruit trees, including longans, lychees, and starfruits, are abundant in the New Territories.

Some of the oldest areas of woodlands are the *Feng Shui* (fung soy) woods, or sacred groves found near villages in the New Territories. Villagers have protected these forests because they believe that the trees improve the spiritual and luck-bringing quality of the environment.

FAUNA

TERRESTRIAL MAMMALS Ongoing urbanization has severely disrupted the quiet rhythm of the countryside. Wild mammals are rapidly disappearing from Hong Kong. Occasionally civets, foxes, Chinese leopard cats, and

TYPHOONS

In Hong Kong typhoons (also known as tropical cyclones or hurricanes) occur mainly between July and October. About five or six typhoons affect Hong Kong each year. The torrential downpours and strong winds that usually accompany typhoons sometimes cause great destruction to life and property. Some of the most destructive typhoons that have hit Hong Kong include Wanda (1962), Ellen (1983), Wayne (1986), and Brenda (1989).

In the past, when Hong Kong was not as developed as it is today, major typhoons resulted in many casualties. Today improved structure design and engineering provide better shelter, which results in fewer casualties. Fishing communities are protected by special typhoon shelters, such as the one at Aberdeen (*above*). However, the economic loss caused by typhoons is immeasurable. For example, when a typhoon warning is issued, traffic becomes even more chaotic than usual. Commuting becomes almost impossible, and valuable work hours are lost. Hong Kong's observatory works in close communication with the major transportation operators and other government departments to ensure a state of preparedness for typhoons.

Despite all the problems they cause the typhoons bring rains that contribute to the water supply in Hong Kong. They provide relief from the oppressive heat of a long summer, as well as a welcome day of rest for everyone except the meteorologists and emergency service workers.

ISLAND ATTRACTIONS

LANTAU ISLAND *(below)*, also known as Tai Yue Shan, is nearly double the size of Hong Kong Island, but with almost a million fewer residents, it is as peaceful as Hong Kong is hurried. However, recent years have witnessed the development of new housing and leisure facilities on Lantau Island. The largest settlement is called Tai O.

Lantau's main attraction is the Po Lin (Precious Lotus) Monastery, with its beautiful Buddhist temple. The monastery was established by monks from China in the 1950s. In 1991 the Po Lin monks completed the largest statue of Buddha in Asia. It weighs 250 tons (254 metric tons) and stands 112 feet (34 m) tall.

Cheung Chau, which lies to the southeast of Lantau Island, has a somewhat Mediterranean air to it. Two intriguing old temples attract tourists, but locals go there just to walk through the streets, where cars are banned. The island is also known for its excellent seafood restaurants. Although densely populated Cheung Chau has a relaxed atmosphere that makes it seem less crowded than it really is. A cave at the southern end of the island that was once used by the notorious local pirate Cheung Po Tsai hosts the famous Bun Festival every year in May.

Chinese porcupines may be seen in the New Territories. Leopards and tigers have not been seen for many years. The Barking Deer, a small deer that barks like a dog at night, is now heard only infrequently in wooded areas and is seen even less frequently. Rhesus macaques (a type of monkey), long-tailed macaques, and squirrels can also be found in wooded areas.

BIRDS The Hong Kong Bird Watching Society lists 431 species of birds that have been recorded in the wild during the past 50 years. The Yim Tso Ha bird sanctuary, near Starling Inlet, provides a home for herons and egrets. The Mai Po Marshes—an area of mudflats, mangroves, and shrimp ponds in the north—are the richest habitat for birds in Hong Kong.

AQUATIC LIFE Hong Kong has a very diverse marine life. There are an estimated 1,800 different species of fishes in the South China Sea. Clupeoids, croakers, and sea bream are frequently found around Hong Kong. Corals, shelled mollusks, crustaceans, and cephalopods are also common. Marine mammals as well as the Chinese white dolphin, the black finless porpoise, and the bottlenose dolphin are protected under Hong Kong's Wild Animals Protection Ordinance. The green turtle is the only known species of sea turtle that breeds locally.

SNAKES Hong Kong has its share of poisonous snakes, such as kraits, coral snakes, cobras, and vipers. However, most snakes in Hong Kong are harmless.

Daring monkeys venture around the Kowloon reservoirs, hoping to pick up scraps of food from picnickers.

13

THE GREEN SEA TURTLE

The green sea turtle has a shell that comes in a variety of colors—olive brown, dark green, gray, or even black. The green sea turtle is the largest hard-shelled sea turtle in the world and it is named for its greenish-colored fat. This greenish tint is the result of the turtle's vegetarian diet. Unlike its marine counterparts the green sea turtle is herbivorous, feasting on seagrass and algae.

An adult green sea turtle can grow to more than 3 feet (0.91 m) long and can weigh around 350 pounds (159 kg).

These coastal inhabitants have been sighted in the Atlantic and Pacific oceans. Globally endangered, the number of mature females has declined by 65 percent in the last 100 years. In 2002 the discovery of two turtles nesting in Sham Wan generated much excitement among Hong Kongers.

CITIES, NEW TOWNS, VILLAGES

CENTRAL DISTRICT The City of Victoria—formerly the capital of Hong Kong—is always referred to by Hong Kongers as the "Central District," or simply "Central." It is on the northwest coast of Hong Kong Island and has been the center of administrative and economic activities in the territory since the British settlement in 1841.

Central's dramatic skyscrapers, colonial buildings, and streets lined with shops are constructed on a strip of land along the coast and along the foothills of the mountains behind. Central's stunning view of Victoria Harbor, the city, and the mountains has been immortalized in various paintings and photographs.

KOWLOON On the other side of the harbor is the Kowloon Peninsula, which has undergone great development in recent years. Hong Kong's Kai Tak Airport is located on the eastern fringe of the peninsula. Tsim Sha Tsui, on the tip of the peninsula, is a bustling shopping and nightlife district. Factories, businesses, apartment houses, shops, and markets compete for space. As the peninsula is gradually becoming more crowded, the urban area is spreading northward into the New Kowloon area.

NEW TOWNS As a result of housing pressures on Hong Kong Island and the Kowloon Peninsula, several new towns have been built in the New Territories. These include Tsuen Wan, Tuen Mun, Sha Tin, Tai Po, Fanling, and Yuen Long. Over one-quarter of Hong Kong's population lives in the New Territories, and over three-quarters of these people live in the new towns. The residents of the densely populated high-rise apartments are catered to by shops, schools, transportation systems, and other services.

SMALL TOWNS AND VILLAGES A more traditional style of living continues to exist in villages and small towns. Most of the villages follow the alignment of the river valleys in the New Territories.

A walled village in the New Territories.

HISTORY

HONG KONG'S history has been shaped primarily by two powers: Britain and China. Until the 19th century Hong Kong was nothing more than a rocky, sparsely inhabited island off the coast of China. Its modern history began when the British established a settlement on Hong Kong Island in order to initiate trade with China. Hong Kong Island, and subsequently Kowloon Peninsula and the New Territories, became part of a British colony.

Hong Kong's growth in the 19th and 20th centuries was dramatic. Lured by economic opportunities, people from mainland China flooded into the colony. Some flocked there to flee from the miseries in their homeland. Despite the outbreaks of war and the Japanese occupation on December 25, 1941, Hong Kong thrived.

Present-day Hong Kong has one very unique characteristic: It is neither completely British nor completely Chinese. The country entered a new era in July 1997, when the British lease on the New Territories expired and Hong Kong reverted to Chinese rule.

During the Ming Dynasty (1368–1644), Hong Kong shipped incense to the Yangzi Valley area. The name of the island, which means "fragrant harbor," came from this incense trade.

Left: **In the 19th century, Hong Kong's harbor was visited by junks (Chinese sailboats) and British vessels. Today junks are a symbol of the old Hong Kong.**

Opposite: **The clock tower of Tsim Sha Tsui, which was built in 1909, remains a legacy of Hong Kong's colonial era.**

A lime kiln in Hong Kong. During the Tang Dynasty, lime was used for caulking wooden boats, waterproofing containers, dressing acidic soil, building, and salt production.

ANCIENT HISTORY

Two Neolithic cultures are believed to have been predominant in the area around Hong Kong from the fourth millennium B.C. Stone tools, pottery, ornaments, and other artifacts have been unearthed in coastal deposits. This suggests that the ancient inhabitants of Hong Kong depended largely on the sea for their survival. There is also evidence of inland settlement. Bronze Age artifacts such as swords, arrowheads, axes, and fishhooks have been found. The discovery of stone molds suggests that the locals worked with metal.

Ancient Chinese literary records refer to a group of maritime people known as the Yue, who occupied China's southeastern coast. The Han Chinese from northern China conquered this region during the Qin (221–206 B.C.) and Han (206 B.C.–A.D. 220) dynasties. Many excavations uncovered coins from the Qin and Han periods. Probably the most outstanding find from this period was the brick tomb that was uncovered at Lei Cheng Uk in Kowloon in 1955. Its architecture follows the typical style of Han tomb furniture. Archaeological finds from later historical periods are rare. The dome-shaped limekilns that dot the territory's beaches suggest the importance of lime as a commodity during the Tang Dynasty (A.D. 618–907).

The first major migration from the north happened during the Song Dynasty (A.D. 960–1279). However, Hong Kong remained sparsely populated until the 19th century. Its coves and islets were ideal hideouts for pirates who plied the South China Sea.

BRITISH TRADE WITH CHINA

In 1553 Portugal established a trading base at Macao, about 40 miles (64 km) away from Hong Kong. Macao quickly became the principal port for international trade with China and Japan.

British merchants began trading with China in the late 1700s. During those days tea imported from Asia had become a favorite drink in England, and the trade was extremely profitable. However, in line with their policy of isolation, the Chinese authorities imposed severe restrictions on the British merchants. They reluctantly allowed a few British merchants to set up offices in the Chinese port of Guangzhou (Canton), but they dictated all transaction terms, accepting only silver and gold in exchange for their tea.

The British soon introduced a new product to tempt the Chinese: opium, a powerful narcotic made from the poppy flower. European sailors brought opium smoking to China in the 1600s. British merchants shipped opium from India to China, where they received gold and silver as payment. By the late 1700s China recorded an estimated two million addicts, and the number was gradually spiraling out of control. Opium addiction drained China's wealth and wreaked havoc across the country. In 1799 China made the opium trade illegal.

In order to get around the trade restrictions imposed by the Chinese, British merchants began to look for a base where they could establish their own trading center. With the outbreak of the Opium Wars in the early 1800s, they got the chance they had been waiting for.

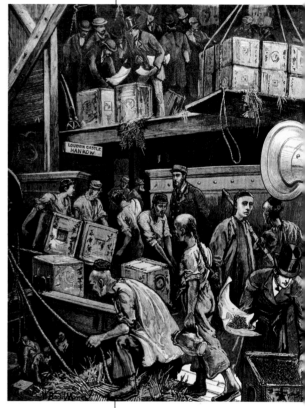

Tea from China being unloaded at a dock in London.

An illustration of a sea battle between the Chinese and British forces. The Opium Wars ended the long period of Chinese isolation from other civilizations.

THE OPIUM WARS

In 1839 Lin Zexu, a Chinese imperial commissioner, was sent to Guangzhou to suppress opium smuggling by British merchants. Lin surrounded the British offices with troops, stopped food supplies, and refused to let anyone leave until all opium stocks were surrendered. After a siege that lasted six weeks, Captain Charles Elliot, the British government trade representative, authorized the surrender of 20,283 opium chests.

This enraged the British merchants, who demanded either a commercial treaty that would put trade relations on a satisfactory footing, or that the Chinese give to the British a small island where the British could live under their own flag, without threats from China. Hostilities came to a head when a Chinese man was killed in a drunken brawl between British sailors and Chinese fishermen. Driven out of China, most of the British escaped to the island of Hong Kong. Fighting soon started between the British and Chinese naval forces along the coast. This signaled the beginning of the First Opium War in 1839.

Given its military might, Britain scored an easy victory. China was forced to open a number of Chinese ports to British trade and residence.

Besides ceding Hong Kong the country also had to grant Britain the right to try British citizens who lived in China only within British courts. The decline of the Qing Dynasty ushered in China's defeat in a series of wars at the hands of other European powers, who then received similar privileges based on their military might.

When the British established their settlement in Hong Kong, it was still a rural backwater. The area had 20 villages and hamlets housing a population of about 4,000. Around 2,000 fisherfolk lived on boats along the harbor. Hong Kong had only two natural assets—a sheltered deepwater harbor and a strategic location along the trade routes of the Far East.

The Nanjing Treaty, which ended the Opium War of 1839 to 1842, opened up more Chinese ports for British trade, dissolved restrictive trade policies, and allowed the British to station ambassadors in China. The Second Opium War was caused by China's continuing objections to the opium trade and disputes over the interpretation of the earlier treaties. A joint offensive by Britain and France resulted in another defeat for China. The Treaty of Tianjin (then called Tientsin) was signed in 1858, but the Chinese authorities refused to ratify it. Hostilities resumed, and the Western allies captured the capital, Beijing (Peking).

In 1860 China agreed to a treaty with Britain that opened 11 more ports, permitted foreign envoys to reside in Beijing, allowed foreigners to travel in the Chinese interior, and legalized the importation of opium. Kowloon was also ceded to Britain. Other European countries and Japan demanded concessions from China, too. Defeated twice in the Opium Wars, China fell into a century-long period of humiliation by foreign powers.

Merchants' offices and warehouses line the Hong Kong waterfront during the late 19th century.

GROWTH OF THE COLONY

After China's defeat in the first Sino-Japanese War (1894–95), Britain demanded control of the land around Hong Kong for defensive purposes. On June 9, 1898, the New Territories—the area north of the Kowloon Peninsula up to the Sham Chun River, along with 233 outlying islands—was leased to Britain for 99 years. The British faced some opposition when they took over the New Territories, but it soon subsided.

The new settlement in Hong Kong faced severe stumbling blocks at first. Fever and typhoons threatened lives and property. Crime was rampant. The population rose from 32,983 (31,463 Chinese) in 1851 to 878,947 (859,425 Chinese) in 1931. After the Qing Dynasty was overthrown in 1911, many people took refuge in Hong Kong, fleeing the misery in China. The British had not anticipated that the Chinese would choose to live under a foreign flag, so the influx of migrants to the territory took the colonial administration by surprise.

Despite an unsteady start the settlement thrived under British rule. Hong Kong became a center of trade with Chinese communities abroad. The late 19th and early 20th centuries saw rapid growth and development in education, health, and social services.

At the end of World War I strong nationalist sentiments awakened when Germany refused to give its Shantung (Shandong) concessions back to China. The unrest spread to Hong Kong. Because it had the largest stake in China, Britain became the main target of antiforeign sentiment, but that soon changed.

Chinese refugees line up for water in 1933. During the 1930s, hundreds and thousands of refugees fled the war with Japan and made their way to Hong Kong, bringing the population at the outbreak of World War II to an estimated 1.6 million.

In 1931 Japan occupied Manchuria and tried to take over China's northern provinces. Open warfare broke out in 1937. This marked the beginning of the Second Sino-Japanese War. Guangzhou fell to the Japanese in 1938, causing a mass flight of refugees to Hong Kong.

WORLD WAR II

Japan entered World War II on December 7, 1941, when its aircraft bombed U.S. warships at Pearl Harbor. At approximately the same time, Japanese aircraft bombed Kowloon, and troops invaded Hong Kong from the Chinese mainland. The Japanese attack forced the British to withdraw from the New Territories and Kowloon to Hong Kong Island. After a week of dogged resistance the defenders on the island were exhausted, and Hong Kong surrendered to Japan on Christmas Day.

The three years and eight months of Japanese occupation were a terrible time for Hong Kong. Trade virtually ceased, currency lost its value, and the food supply was disrupted. Government services and public utilities were seriously impaired. Many residents fled to China and Macao. Toward the latter part of the occupation, the Japanese attempted to alleviate the food problems by organizing mass deportations to mainland China.

Soon after the Japanese surrender in August 14, 1945, the colonial secretary set up a provisional government. On August 30, Rear Admiral Sir Cecil Harcourt arrived to establish a temporary military government. Civil government was formally restored on May 1, 1946, when Sir Mark Young resumed his interrupted governorship.

A World War II veteran visits the war memorial in the Central District.

23

Vietnamese boat people added to Hong Kong's overall population during the 1970s.

POPULATION GROWTH AND SOCIAL UNREST

With Hong Kong back under British rule once again, those who had fled Hong Kong during the war gradually returned. The population, which had dwindled to about 600,000 in 1945, swelled to 1.8 million by the end of 1947.

From 1948 to 1949, as the forces of the Chinese Nationalist government faced defeat in the civil war against the Communists, hundreds of thousands of people entered the territory. By 1950 the population reached an estimated 2.2 million.

Hong Kong experienced a period of mounting tension in the 1960s. Social unrest and discontent over poor working conditions began to spread. In 1967 severe riots broke out following a labor dispute at a factory. Inspired by the Cultural Revolution that was sweeping through China, localized unrest soon turned into violent political demonstrations. The disruption affected all aspects of life and temporarily paralyzed the economy. However, by the end of the year, the disturbances had been contained. Legislation improved labor conditions and Hong Kong continued to progress peacefully.

RETURN TO CHINA

As the British lease on the New Territories neared its expiration date in 1997, concern grew about the territory's future. Formal negotiations between Britain and China commenced in 1982, when British Prime Minister Margaret Thatcher visited Beijing. In 1984 a Sino-British Joint Declaration was signed by the heads of both governments. The agreement stipulated that all of Hong Kong would be returned to China on July 1, 1997. The Chinese government agreed to establish a self-governing Special Administrative Region under its central government. According to the terms of the Joint Declaration the current social and economic systems would remain unchanged for the next 50 years, until 2047.

Signs like this started appearing in Hong Kong in the years leading up to the reversion back to Chinese rule.

GOVERNMENT

THE GOVERNMENT OF HONG KONG has experienced a period of great upheaval. Until June 30, 1997, Hong Kong had been a colony of the United Kingdom. A governor nominated in London served as the representative of Queen Elizabeth II. An Executive Council and Legislative Council, which were also nominated rather than elected, decided matters of policy and controlled expenditures.

On July 1, 1997, when the lease of the New Territories expired, Hong Kong reverted to Chinese rule. Under the terms of the Sino-British Joint Declaration, which was signed in 1984, Hong Kong is now a Special Administrative Region (SAR) of China.

Above: **Officers on duty at the Chek Lap Kok Airport.**

Opposite: **The Chinese and Hong Kong flags fly side by side, symbolic of the government system in place in present-day Hong Kong.**

Although it is part of the Communist People's Republic of China, the SAR's administration retains many features of the British colonial system. Democratic reforms that were introduced by the British in the 1980s and 1990s have also left their mark on the SAR government.

The transition from British to Chinese rule has raised many questions in the minds of Hong Kongers. Issues of self-determination, democracy, nationalism, and cultural identity have been actively debated, and tensions have sometimes erupted into angry protests. Some Hong Kong residents greeted the return to Chinese rule with patriotic enthusiasm, while others were apprehensive about the social and economic changes that would result. Some Hong Kongers rushed to obtain British passports to ensure that they would be able to go to Britain if living in the new Hong Kong became too difficult. Others emigrated to the United States, Canada, Australia, and other countries. A decade later many Hong Kongers have realized that life under Chinese rule is not as disruptive as was initially feared.

THE COLONIAL GOVERNMENT

The current government of Hong Kong is based on the former colonial system. As a British colony Hong Kong was administered by the Hong Kong government, which was headed by a governor who was a representative of England's Queen Elizabeth II. An Executive Council offered advice to the governor on important matters of policy. A Legislative Council (known as LegCo) passed laws, controlled public expenditures, and monitored the performance of the government. Two municipal councils (the Urban Council and the Regional Council) provided public health, cultural, and recreational services, and 18 district boards provided a forum for public consultation.

Until 1985 the governor was appointed by the monarch from England, the Executive Council was appointed by the governor, and the members of LegCo were selected by the governor and the British government. There were no democratic elections. Power was concentrated in the hands of business and political elites, many of whom were expatriates. It was often said that the Hong Kong had a laissez-faire government, which means that government intervention in economic matters was minimal. Most Hong Kongers were happy to get on with business and not worry about politics.

THE PEOPLE'S REPUBLIC OF CHINA

Across the border, in mainland China, a very different system was operating. The People's Republic of China (PRC) is a communist republic. The Chinese Communist Party (CCP) controls all major governmental

Above: **Symbols of British rule, once common in Hong Kong, are now removed. w**

Opposite: **The Legislative Council building lies behind a water fountain, while the Bank of China building gleams in the background.**

institutions. Although China has a legislative body—the National People's Congress—real power lies in the hands of the CCP and the State Council, which are the top executive government organs.

When the CCP came to power in China in 1949, it instituted a communist economic system with central planning, state-run industries, and collectivized agriculture. In an effort to abolish the old social and economic systems, private enterprise and religion were banned. The centralized control of the economy ran counter to Hong Kong's system, which was built on free enterprise and minimal government involvement in trade and industry.

In the 1970s the Chinese government began to introduce economic reforms and encourage foreign investment and trade. However, China continues to be criticized for its repression of dissidents and its unwillingness to adopt democratic reforms.

For much of Hong Kong's history the Chinese and British governments tolerated one another and benefited from cross-border trade, even during times of political tension. However, the different styles of government, particularly their approaches to economic affairs, became a major issue in the 1980s and 1990s.

THE TRANSITIONAL PHASE

". . . the Government of the People's Republic of China will resume the exercise of sovereignty over Hong Kong with effect from 1 July 1997, thus fulfilling the long-cherished aspiration of the Chinese people for the recovery of Hong Kong."

—Yang Shangkun, president of the People's Republic of China, in the preamble to the Basic Law

When Britain and China began negotiating the terms of Hong Kong's reversion to China in the early 1980s, Hong Kongers were made painfully aware of how little say they had in the administration of their territory. Many people felt that Hong Kong was being handed over from one master to another without any input from the people who lived there.

In response to calls for greater participation, the Sino-British Joint Declaration stated that the Legislative Council of the SAR would be elected, but the details of the system were not specified. The first election for the legislature was held in 1985, but only for a minority of seats. Although the Chinese government was unsympathetic toward these belated democratic reforms, the transition seemed to be progressing smoothly.

Meanwhile the Chinese government prepared the Basic Law that would be the mini-constitution of the SAR. Released on April 4, 1990, in the wake of the Tiananmen Square massacre, the Basic Law went into effect on July 1, 1997. The Basic Law made it clear that there would be no territory-wide, freely held elections for all seats. Only one-third of the members of the Legislative Council would be directly elected.

Despite the apprehension that this caused among Hong Kongers, democratic reforms were proceeding in the colony. Political parties were formed, and an election was held in 1991. Prodemocracy candidates won virtually all of the directly elected seats. A new governor, Christopher Patten, was appointed by Britain in 1992. Patten increased the power of the Legislative Council and introduced other political reforms despite objections from Beijing. In response the Chinese authorities announced that they would dissolve LegCo in July 1997 and replace it with a provisional Legislative Council.

In March 1993 the Chinese government announced the members of a Preliminary Working Committee, a shadow government that consisted of prominent PRC and Hong Kong political, judicial, and professional figures. As July 1997 drew closer and people began to accept the inevitable reversion to China, support for Patten and his reforms declined.

Above: **Christopher Patten, the last British governor of Hong Kong.**

Opposite: **The locals gather to commemorate the Tiananmen Square massacre.**

THE TIANANMEN SQUARE MASSACRE

The political atmosphere in Hong Kong changed suddenly on June 4, 1989, when thousands of people protesting in Tiananmen Square in Beijing, China, were killed, injured, or imprisoned by government soldiers. Known as the Tiananmen Square massacre, the incident caused a furor in Hong Kong. Hundreds of thousands of Hong Kongers filled the streets in protest. Many Hong Kongers supported the dissidents in China, sending money or helping them escape from China. Hong Kongers feared that freedom of speech and other rights would be lost when China took control of Hong Kong. It was in this turbulent atmosphere that the Basic Law was completed.

ONE COUNTRY, TWO SYSTEMS

The principle of the Special Administrative Region is summed up in the phrase "one country, two systems." According to the Sino-British agreement the PRC's socialist system and policies will not be practiced in Hong Kong within the next 50 years. A public education program (*above*) has kept people informed about the transition.

The main elements of the agreement are as follows:

- The existing economic and social systems will continue.
- Free movement of goods and capital, and Hong Kong's status as a free port and separate customs territory, will be ensured.
- Hong Kong will continue to determine its own monetary and financial policies.
- No taxes will be paid to China.
- The Hong Kong dollar will continue to be freely convertible.
- Property rights and foreign investment will be protected.
- The British common law system will be retained, and fundamental human rights will be protected by law.
- The judiciary will remain independent.

THE SPECIAL ADMINISTRATIVE REGION

As the leader of Hong Kong's government the chief executive is appointed by the PRC government in Beijing to serve for a maximum of two five-year terms. In 1996 Tung Chee Hwa was chosen as the SAR's first chief executive. A shipping magnate who had served as a consultant to both the Hong Kong and PRC governments, Tung was considered politically neutral. However, his governance generated widespread dissatisfaction. Tung resigned in 2005, citing health reasons. Donald Tsang completed Tung's remaining tenure before going on to win a full five-year term of his own in 2007.

Under the plans outlined during the transition period the chief executive will appoint the Executive Council, the administration secretary, the financial secretary, and the secretary of justice. The Legislative Council has 60 members. Twenty of these were directly elected, and the number grew to 30 by 2007. The Legislative Council oversees the day-to-day running of Hong Kong, while the State Council in Beijing handles defense and foreign affairs.

The Chinese government is unlikely to introduce further democratic reforms. It prefers to retain a system based on consultation rather than democratic consent. Since the SAR's top echelon consists of privileged business tycoons, many Hong Kongers believe that their ruling elite are out of touch with popular sentiments.

Tung Chee Hwa, first and former chief executive of Hong Kong.

ECONOMY

HONG KONG IS ADVANCED in manufacturing, trade, and shipping. It is also a regional financial center and serves as an agent in China's pursuit of modernization. Sustained government policies of free enterprise, free trade, and low taxation have created a thriving commercial hub. The territory has been considered the world's freest economy for many years. Its transportation infrastructure is also increasingly sophisticated.

During the 1990s, as Hong Kong's reversion to Chinese rule drew closer, the business community was apprehensive about how Hong Kong's free-market economy would mesh with China's centralized system. Multinational corporations wondered whether they should pull out of Hong Kong and relocate elsewhere in Asia. China put most of these fears to rest with the announcement that Hong Kong's economic system will remain intact for the next 50 years.

Signed in 2003 China's Close Economic Partnership Agreement (CEPA) with the SAR does not tax goods that originate in Hong Kong, making the territory's products more attractive to Chinese consumers than a lot of foreign merchandise.

Left: **A typical day on the busy streets of Aberdeen, Hong Kong.**

Opposite: **This gleaming Bank of China building was designed by the famous American-Chinese architect I. M. Pei. It stands at nearly 300 meters, and is 70 stories high.**

An oil terminal and power station located on Tsing Yi Island.

A LACK OF RESOURCES

Hong Kong is dependent on imports for virtually all of its requirements, such as food, raw materials, consumer goods, capital goods, and fuel. Even water is in short supply. Despite Hong Kong's many reservoirs a substantial proportion of the water consumed by the territory is imported from mainland China.

Hong Kong has no mineral resources to speak of. Graphite and lead mining at Cham Sham (or Needle Hill) and iron ore extraction at Ma On Shan ceased years ago. Small quantities of feldspar are produced for domestic consumption.

Given Hong Kong's sparse forest cover, commercial timber felling is unviable, and there is no potential for producing hydroelectric power from Hong Kong's small streams.

AGRICULTURE AND FISHING

As only 5 percent of the land area is arable, agriculture in Hong Kong is limited. Out of this about 40 percent is abandoned or fallow. Less than 3 percent of the population is made up of farmers. Rice cultivation has been replaced by intensive vegetable and pond fish farming, which provide a much greater return on investment. Greenhouse production of fruits, flowers, sweet potatoes, and melons is done in the New Territories.

Marine fishing is conducted in the waters around Hong Kong. Fishponds occupy 2 percent of the land, and a marine fish culture industry is located in the eastern New Territories.

Lemons are laid out in the sun to dry.

Hong Kong is one of the major air and sea transportation hubs in Asia.

TRADE AND TOURISM

Hong Kong is one of the world's great trade centers because there is no tariff on imports, except on certain luxury goods such as perfumes, cars, gasoline, alcohol, and tobacco.

Almost half of Hong Kong's trade activity consists of imports—generally raw materials and industrial parts. Clothing, food, machinery, and other consumer goods are also imported, primarily from China and Japan. Other major suppliers include the United States, Taiwan, Singapore, the United Kingdom, South Korea, and Germany.

The United States is Hong Kong's main export market. Other major markets include China, the United Kingdom, Germany, Japan, and Canada. Re-exports—goods that are imported from one country and immediately exported to another—account for the majority of goods that are shipped from Hong Kong.

Hong Kong is also a major tourist site, with a recorded 28 million visitors in 2007. Hong Kong's popularity as an international conference and exhibition site means that almost one-third of its visitors are business travelers. Tourism is the third-largest source of foreign exchange earnings.

TRANSPORTATION

Because there are limited roads that serve Hong Kong's dense population, the government imposes strict restrictions on car ownership. Compared to other Asian cities, in Hong Kong the number of cars is extremely low. However, there are still enough vehicles to cause traffic jams, which have become a part of commuting life in the Central District and Kowloon.

Most commuters use the well-developed public transportation system. An ultraefficient subway known as the Mass Transit Railway (MTR) connects Hong Kong Island with Kowloon and the New Territories. Passenger and freight rail services to Guangzhou are also available. Other forms of public transportation include buses and electric trolleys. Cable cars operate between Victoria Peak and the Central District, while ferries (*below*) shuttle people between mainland China and Hong Kong's major islands.

Located on the eastern fringe of Kowloon, Hong Kong's Kai Tak Airport used to be one of the busiest airports in the world. In 1995 more than 27.4 million passengers passed through it. However, Kai Tak could not accommodate increased air traffic. So a new airport was built at Chek Lap Kok, an islet to the north of Lantau Island. Opened in 1998 Chek Lap Kok Airport serves 87 million passengers and handles 9.9 million tons (8,981,128,926 kg) of cargo annually. The inauguration of this airport provided much relief from noise pollution that residents who lived within Kai Tak's flight path had suffered.

Above: **Hong Kong is well known for its busy shipping industries.**

Opposite: **The Lippo Center in the Central District houses many financial offices.**

INDUSTRY AND MANUFACTURING

As an international duty-free port Hong Kong flourished commercially until 1951, when the United Nations (UN) placed an embargo on trade with Communist China and North Korea. Chinese industrialists, many of them from Shanghai, avoided the UN embargo by immigrating to Hong Kong. They brought with them the technology, skilled labor, and capital that catalyzed Hong Kong's rapid industrial development.

Trade between Hong Kong and China later revived. Foreign investment flowed in as manufacturers took advantage of the territory's cheap, abundant labor and the low cost of raw materials from China. In the 1980s the manufacturing sector employed almost 40 percent of the labor force and became the most important part of Hong Kong's economy. However, its significance declined a decade later. Attracted by lower costs, businesses shifted base to Guangzhou and other Chinese cities. By 2004 manufacturing contributed only 4 percent to Hong Kong's economy.

Emphasis shifted to the production of value-added goods, such as electronics, which require better-skilled labor and command premium prices. The service sector grew to become the gateway to southern China. Hong Kong continues to conduct export operations for facilities that have relocated to the mainland.

Hong Kong's strategic position on major shipping and aviation routes led the territory to develop transportation-related heavy industries. Today Hong Kong enjoys an international reputation in shipbuilding and aircraft engineering.

FINANCIAL SERVICES

Hong Kong has developed into the leading financial center in Asia. It ranks third in the world, after New York and London. There is no central bank: The major commercial banks and the government-run Banking Commissioner's Office work together to manage the territory's currency and interest rates.

Hong Kong's probusiness environment is reflected in its sophisticated financial infrastructure. A wide range of services is easily available, and there are no restrictions on foreign exchange. Such features have attracted many foreign banks, and 85 of the world's 100 largest banks are represented in the territory.

Domestic and international currencies are traded at the Hong Kong foreign exchange market. The fifth largest in the world, it has a daily turnover of over $90 billion.

Although Hong Kong's commercial openness is a draw, Hong Kong is vulnerable to regional fluctuations and global changes. In 1998 the Asian financial crisis battered many currencies, including the Thai *baht* and Korean *won*, but the Hong Kong dollar suffered only a slight drop in value. This can be attributed to the territory's large foreign reserves, which cushioned the Hong Kong currency from the crisis.

ENVIRONMENT

HONG KONG'S ENVIRONMENT has suffered from the territory's rapid development. Black smoke billows incessantly from power plants. Factories dump chemical wastes into open waters. Construction sites emit noise and dust around the clock. Collectively they lead to serious air and water pollution.

Both the local and expatriate communities fret over Hong Kong's deteriorating quality of life. The territory's worsening air quality is a source of concern. Shrinking marine biodiversity is another worry. To address such problems the government has implemented various laws. Ongoing conservation efforts seek to boost ecological awareness among the general public. However, more needs to be done at the grassroots level before Hong Kong can thoroughly clean up its environmental track record.

Hong Kong is party to several international agreements, including those that govern marine dumping and ship pollution.

Left: **A ferry in Sai Kung harbor travels toward Hong Kong Island.**

Opposite: **Much of Hong Kong's lush forests have been cleared to construct modern buildings.**

SOIL EROSION

Hong Kong's rugged terrain and high population pressures mean there is little land available for cultivation. Only 5 percent of the territory is considered arable. The original forest vegetation had already been cut or burned by the 1800s. Wooded hills cover only one-fifth of Hong Kong, while grasslands, badlands, and swamps account for over half of the territory's total area.

The region's heavy rainfall makes matters worse. Sparse vegetation and limited forest canopy expose unprotected land to frequent downpours. Nutrients are leached from the soil, making it poor and unsuitable for agriculture. With no plant roots to bind the earth, large tracts of land are easily weakened and swept away. During summer, soil erosion on slopes occurs regularly. Roads and drainage systems are blocked, leading to floods, property damage, business losses, and severe inconvenience for the local people.

CONFLICTING LAND USE

In land-scarce Hong Kong, it is common to see old industrial buildings jostling for space with residential apartments. Vehicle repair workshops and potentially hazardous sites, such as cement works, often border housing estates. Such development highlights Hong Kong's lack of proper planning. Controlling conflicting land usage is challenging because of limited legislative powers.

The Ma Tau district in Kowloon is a prime example. The area used to house developments that were at odds with one another. High-rise homes towered over ground-level workshops and garages, or stood adjacent to factories. A few even had an old gas plant as their neighbor. Given the district's proximity to Kai Tak Airport, the town planning board has promoted redevelopment by encouraging warehouses and offices in the airfreight industry to locate here.

Many of the factories emit harmful chemicals, causing the air to be increasingly polluted.

AIR POLLUTION

Like any large urban city Hong Kong faces immense threats from air pollution. Vehicle emissions, especially from diesel-fueled engines, are a pressing problem. Factories in the Pearl River delta spew pollutants that often blanket the region in smog. Since the late 1990s Hong Kong's Air Pollution Index has regularly exceeded the dangerous level of 100.

To control air pollution the government has encouraged the use of cleaner fuels and vehicles. In 2005 nearly all of the territory's 18,000 taxis and light buses switched to liquefied petroleum gas (LPG)—a cleaner

Hong Kong's eastern beaches are cleaner than the others because they are farther away from the polluted Pearl River delta. Even so it may be wise to check beach pollution reports beforehand if you are visiting Hong Kong, so that your seaside vacation plans do not run aground.

alternative to conventional diesel fuel. Hong Kong is also the first Asian economy to sell ultra-low-sulfur diesel, a motor fuel that releases fewer sulfur dioxide pollutants. Financial incentives are given to people who use environmentally friendly modes of transportation.

Besides diesel vehicles, electricity-generating power plants add pollutants to the air. The Environment Protection Department (EPD) caps the emission levels of furnace installations and large industrial facilities.

Unfortunately there are no easy solutions for the regional smog problem. Many Hong Kong businesses have factory operations in nearby Guangzhou, which blatantly flout environmental regulations. To combat air pollution on a larger scale, the government has initiated regional tie-ups with southern Chinese cities.

WEATHER FORECAST—BLUE SKIES AHEAD?

The Hong Kong government has dished out various cash perks to ensure cleaner air. Rail operators get priority funding. Tax cuts are given for registered cars that comply with the European Union's Euro IV emission standards. Owners of diesel-operated vehicles enjoy subsidies when they install particulate traps.

Environmentally damaging practices are punishable offenses. The number of smoky vehicles plunged by 80 percent when the size of the fines against them increased from $58 to $128. By 2006 the amount of suspended particulates in urban areas had been successfully cut to 20 percent of the 1999 level.

The authorities launched an "Action Blue Sky" campaign in mid-2006 to improve air quality. Corporations and schools pledged to conserve energy by maintaining indoor room temperatures at 77°F (25°C) in summer. A "Dress Down in Summer" campaign also tried to reduce the community's dependence on air conditioning.

NOISE POLLUTION

City dwellers worldwide suffer from noise problems, including road traffic noise. Hong Kongers probably face worse noise than many of their global counterparts. Hong Kong's narrow streets, densely built-up spaces, and constant human activities generate a constant cacophony every day.

Direct measures to reduce the excessive din include adjusting road alignment, resurfacing roads with low-noise materials, and erecting noise barriers. Legislation was tightened in 2002 to ensure that new vehicles complied with internationally recognized noise standards. Permits for construction regulate the use of heavy equipment at night and during public holidays to alleviate the problem.

Noise produced by aircraft was a nuisance for Kowloon City residents who lived near Kai Tak Airport. However, the completion of Chek Lap Kok Airport, off Lantau Island, has largely resolved this problem.

Trash washed up on a beach on Lamma Island.

WATER QUALITY AND SEWAGE TREATMENT

Water quality in Hong Kong's assorted rivers and bays is erratic. Small streams and tributaries around water catchment areas are cleaner than larger water bodies, such as Inner Deep Bay and Victoria Harbor. The territory's expected population growth—to 8.3 million by 2033—would put greater pressure on water quality.

Untreated sewage that is dumped into open waterways pollutes the numerous seas and bays that surround Hong Kong. In addition to having a bad stench, bacteria in the water can make swimmers ill, contaminate aquatic life, and kill marine species. Pollution from agricultural runoff and human activities also breeds red tides. These toxic algae infestations have wiped out varieties of fish that used to swim near the main islands.

This has forced fishermen to venture farther from shore in search of their catch.

To improve water quality the Environment Protection Department (EPD) controls the wastewater discharge. Factories have to meet specified discharge standards before they are given a license to continue disposal operations. Established in 2001, the Harbor Area Treatment Scheme (HATS) delivers sewage from Victoria Harbor to Stonecutters Island for disinfection and for chemical and biological treatment. A similar system in Tolo Harbor has reduced the occurrence of red tides. About 70 percent of the sewage produced daily is treated.

The drive to improve Hong Kong's water quality has been moderately successful. However, periodic red tide outbreaks at beaches—41 red tides were recorded in 2005 alone—suggest that Hong Kong still has some way to go before its water resources can be given a completely clean bill of health.

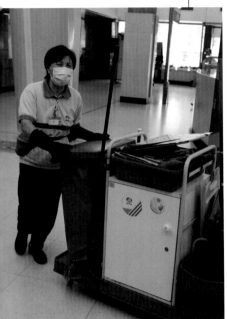

Hong Kong takes pride in its efficient handling of public waste.

WASTE MANAGEMENT

The average Hong Konger disposes of 2.97 pounds (1.35 kg) of garbage daily. About two-thirds of the solid waste generated daily is household trash. The remaining one-third consists of nonhazardous industrial and commercial refuse. The garbage is sent to three landfills in the New Territories, which are estimated to reach full capacity by 2015.

To minimize public health risks the government oversees clinical waste disposal. Chemical waste is treated on Tsing Yi Island, while construction dregs are delivered to mainland China for reclamation projects. In 2005 alone 2.6 tons (2.4 million metric tons) of waste materials such paper, plastics, and metals were exported, generating $4.5 billion.

THE RECYCLING EFFORT

Hong Kong lacks proper facilities for recycling. A 49-acre (20-hectare) ecopark in Tuen Mun will be completed by 2009. The collection, reprocessing, and export of recyclables are undertaken by private enterprises, which are often hampered by inadequate logistics, financing, and infrastructural support.

To encourage individual households to separate waste that can be recycled, voluntary organizations work with the Food and Environmental Hygiene Department (FEHD) to build recycling bins at public parks, commuting points, and building entrances. However, governmental support for such initiatives is patchy. For example, the administration ignored the paper recycling industry's pleas for economic assistance in 1998.

Public agencies can endorse the green movement by being more proactive toward resource conservation and producing less waste. Providing economic incentives for people to recycle more and discard less is another option. Advancing the concept of environmental citizenship, both from the top down and at the grassroots level, takes time, but the rewards are long-term.

Used cans in Hong Kong are usually packed for recycling purposes.

PROTECTED AREAS

Country parks cover 160.6 square miles (416 square km), or almost 40 percent of Hong Kong's total land area. Many scenic hills and woodlands are planted with fire-resistant trees such as acacia and eucalyptus. Development is tightly controlled around these areas. Litter is collected frequently. Educational and recreational facilities, such as hiking trails and camping sites, are clearly marked. Public appreciation of the countryside is obvious in the number of visitors—about 12 million people flocked to these parks in 2004.

Hong Kong's government has spent $1.6 billion on sewage schemes since 1991. It plans to spend another $0.6 billion on such amenities from 2005 to 2010.

49

People enjoying a walking trail through the Hong Kong Wetland Park of Tin Shui Wai, located in the New Territories.

Although smaller in scale Hong Kong's four marine parks and its sole marine reserve are no less important. Spread over 6,005 acres (2,430 hectares) the coastal areas and seascapes sustain a host of conservation and research studies. Fishing is completely banned in the marine reserve. Only local villagers are permitted to fish within marine parks.

ECOFRIENDLY LEGISLATION

Hong Kong has several laws to protect nature. The Agriculture, Fisheries and Conservation Department (AFCD) has the job of conserving ecological resources and enforcing legislation.

Entry to wildlife habitats such as the Mai Po Marshes, Sham Wan, and Yim Tso Ha Egretry is heavily restricted. The sale, export, and possession of protected animal species are prohibited. Rare plants such as azaleas and Hong Kong's native bauhinias are guarded under the Forests and Countryside Ordinance. The use of explosives, toxic substances, or other destructive fishing practices is illegal.

Hikers can choose from any of the "big four" hiking trails—MacLehose, Wilson, Lantau, and Hong Kong— for a dose of nature and solitude.

REGIONAL COOPERATION

A number of cross-boundary plans are currently in the works. The Hong Kong government has partnered with Guangdong's provincial government to tackle the regional smog problem. In 2002 both sides agreed to drastically reduce emissions of four major air pollutants—sulfur dioxide, nitrogen oxide, respirable suspended particulates, and volatile organic compounds—by 2010.

Joint water pollution control efforts are also under way. A plan to clean up Deep Bay was conceived in 2000. Three years later both parties formulated a regional water-quality management strategy to control pollution in Mirs Bay. Present projects include the development of an analytical model to measure the water condition in the Pearl River estuary.

Environmental organizations based in Hong Kong include the Conservancy Association, Friends of the Earth (HK), Green Student Council, Lights Out Hong Kong, and Society for the Protection of the Harbor.

HONG KONG WETLAND PARK

To promote environmental appreciation among the public, Hong Kong opened its first major green tourism facility in 2006. The Wetland Park at Tin Shui Wai reconstructs the natural habitats of waterfowl, native species, and other types of wildlife. Spanning a 148-acre (60-hectare) Wetland Reserve and Wetland Interactive World, it expects to draw more than a million nature lovers annually.

The attraction offers intimate peeks into Hong Kong's ecological diversity. Visitors can step into the world of the green turtle, or watch the endangered black-faced spoonbill bird take flight. Many people also drop by to greet the park's reptilian resident, a female crocodile that is affectionately named Pui Pui, which means "precious one" in Cantonese. The crocodile rules over a deluxe home that is equipped with a heated pool, a landscaped enclosure, and weighing scales.

HONG KONGERS

HONG KONG SOCIETY WAS multiracial from the very start, a reflection of the diverse nature of the British Empire. For example, when Britain took possession of Hong Kong in 1841, there were almost 3,000 Indian soldiers among the British troops.

Since then Hong Kong has absorbed people from all over the world. The ethnic Chinese form the majority of the population. There is, of course, also a British community. In its early days Hong Kong also attracted immigrants from the United States, Germany, Portugal, and Denmark, as well as Hindus, Muslims, Parsis, and Sikhs from India, and Jews from Iraq. There are also Hong Kong–born Eurasians, people of mixed European and Asian heritage.

The original communities that populated Hong Kong boasted people from all walks of life. They were traders, lawyers, missionaries, shipbuilders, shopkeepers, soldiers, journalists, editors, bankers, and artists. Many of

Left: **A businessman in his convertible. He is one of many Hong Kong people who enjoy the benefits of living in a thriving city.**

Opposite: **Hong Kong locals lead very hectic city lifestyles.**

their descendants live in Hong Kong today. They are equally fluent in English and Cantonese. A turbaned Sikh man speaking fluent Cantonese would not merit a second glance in Hong Kong. Smaller communities have managed to keep their distinct identities and traditions alive while adapting to the dominant culture.

Today Hong Kong has a population of around 7 million. About 98 percent of the population is ethnic Chinese, and the remaining 2 percent is evenly divided between Asians and non-Asians.

The territory has a population density of around 17,400 people per square mile (6,700 per square km). Some sections, such as Kowloon's Mong Kok district, house 40,000 people per square mile (100,000 per square km), making them the most densely populated areas on Earth.

THE HONG KONG CHINESE

The overwhelming majority of Hong Kongers are Chinese. About one-third of Hong Kong Chinese were born in China. The Chinese population can be subdivided into groups based on which part of China they (or their ancestors) came from, and which dialect they speak.

CANTONESE Most of the early Chinese immigrants came from the southern Chinese province of Guangdong. They brought with them their dialect, Cantonese, and their customs. Hundreds of thousands of immigrants from Guangdong entered Hong Kong during the first half of the 20th century. Today around 90 percent of Hong Kong Chinese are of Cantonese descent.

Over the years the Hong Kong Chinese have created their own identity, which sets them apart from the Chinese of China or Taiwan. Because they have lived under British influence for so many years, they are perceived as being more Westernized. The Hong Kong Chinese were enjoying the material benefits of modernization, such as television and indoor plumbing, long before these things were available in China or Taiwan. However, this modern veneer has not eliminated their cultural attitudes and traditions, which continue to remain very Chinese.

When Hong Kong was a British colony the Hong Kong Chinese asserted their distinct identity by retaining their Cantonese dialect, rather than adopting Putonghua, the national language of China and Taiwan, which is based on Mandarin, the dialect spoken in Beijing and other parts of China. They also refused to adopt the simplified Chinese characters used in China. However, following the handover to China, the Hong Kong Chinese have started to learn Putonghua and are now using simplified characters in addition to traditional characters.

A Chinese tailor in his garment shop.

OTHER DIALECT GROUPS A minority of Hong Kong Chinese—less than 10 percent—come from other dialect groups. These groups include the Hakka, Siyi, Chaochow, Hoklo, and Tanka. There are also significant numbers of Chinese from Shanghai and Fukien in China, and from Taiwan. There are smaller numbers of people from all over China. Almost all of them live a modern, urban lifestyle, but their heritage is revealed in the dialect they speak among themselves and the details of their cooking,

ceremonies, religious practices, and other customs. The few people who retain a more traditional lifestyle, such as the Hakka farmers of the New Territories, may also have a distinctive style of dress.

OTHER ETHNIC GROUPS

Around 2 percent of the population of Hong Kong belongs to ethnic groups other than Chinese. There are roughly equal numbers of Asians (including Indians, Filipinos, Japanese, and Pakistanis) and non-Asians (including British, Americans, Australians, Canadians, and New Zealanders). Some are descended from early settlers in Hong Kong, while others live in Hong Kong as expatriates (people who live outside their native country by choice).

FOREIGN DEVILS

In Hong Kong, Westerners of Caucasian appearance are referred to as *gweilo* (gwy-loh), which means "foreign devil" in Cantonese.

The ancient Chinese considered China to be the Middle Kingdom, halfway between heaven and hell. Since non-Chinese people could not come from heaven (since that would make them better than the Chinese), they must be from hell; hence, the term *foreign devil*. The Europeans' role in getting millions of Chinese addicted to opium probably reinforced this idea that the Europeans were evil.

Although it is understandably offensive, the term *gweilo* is casually used today, more because it has stayed on as a common reference, rather than an intended insult. It is occasionally even employed as a term of affection.

In Hong Kong the term *expatriate* was once used to describe all non-Chinese, even those who were born in Hong Kong. Ethnic Chinese were not considered foreigners, even if they were born outside of Hong Kong. This attitude changed slowly as Chinese Hong Kongers saw many non-Chinese residents becoming fluent in Cantonese, contributing to the territory's economy and administration.

However, non-Chinese Hong Kongers were made to feel like foreigners in their own land when it was announced that only ethnic Chinese would be given Chinese citizenship in July 1997, when Hong Kong

reverted to China. Some people whose families had been in Hong Kong for generations faced the prospect of becoming stateless. Those who have been fortunate enough to obtain British citizenship are able to remain in the Special Administrative Region. They can leave anytime they want. These people have adopted a wait-and-see attitude. Those who were not so fortunate have had to leave the only home they have ever known, emigrating to the United States, Canada, Singapore, and Malaysia, among other countries.

Top: **The Indian community is one of Hong Kong's oldest minority groups.**

Opposite: **An expatriate waitress at Mad Dog's, an English-style tavern found in Hong Kong.**

INDIANS Indians are a prominent group in Hong Kong's commercial and social scene. In the late 19th and early 20th centuries Indian traders, mostly Dawoodi Bohras from Bombay and the state of Gujarat, came to Hong Kong in large numbers. At first they worked with British traders, and later they set up business for themselves. They were joined by other Indian traders, such as Muslims, Hindus, and Parsis.

Although the traditional occupation of most Hong Kong Indians is trade, the Sikhs usually came to Hong Kong as part of the British police or military force. Even today Sikhs have the reputation of being incorruptible. Hong Kong's organized crime syndicates know that Sikhs cannot be enticed to rob their employers. For this reason, and because they are generally sturdy in their physical build, Sikhs are often employed as guards.

Although most Hong Kong Indians still continue to work in trade, many third- and fourth-generation Hong Kong Indians have

Present-day Hong Kong is a cosmopolitan city with different communities of people living together in harmony.

branched out into other occupations, ranging from academia and banking to the civil service.

JEWS Among the earliest settlers in Hong Kong were Sephardic Jews from Iraq. Sephardic Jews follow the Jewish liturgy and customs of medieval Spain and Portugal. In the 15th century they were expelled from Europe and settled in the Middle East and North Africa.

Iraqi Jews were traders who came to Hong Kong and China by way of India. This merchant community enjoyed close personal and commercial ties with the Jewish communities in Shanghai and Bombay. Initially trading in cotton and other commodities the Jews soon became involved in the opium trade. Eventually they branched out into other areas, including real estate, banking, insurance, and hotels. This propelled them to power and influence, both within Hong Kong and on the international business scene. Lord Lawrence Kadoorie, a member of Hong Kong's Jewish community, was the first person from Hong Kong to have a seat in the United Kingdom's House of Lords.

EURASIANS Eurasian communities can be found in all the Asian countries that were colonized by Europeans. The word *Eurasian* reflects the mixed heritage of those descended from the union of European and Asian parents. Eurasian communities have distinct traditions, cuisine, and customs that differ slightly, depending on the ethnic groups from which they were descended.

Interracial relationships were frowned upon in the early years, and Eurasian children of mixed-race marriages faced considerable discrimination. The separate ethnic communities in Hong Kong were not comfortable with the idea of mixed marriages. However, since Eurasians were usually fluent in English, Cantonese, and possibly the other languages of their parents, the British colonial administration used them to fill posts in the civil service. Many Eurasian families in Hong Kong are among the island's wealthiest and most respected inhabitants.

In recent years a new Eurasian community has grown. Many Hong Kongers have traveled abroad for work or study and have brought home European or American spouses.

Eurasian children on an amusement park ride.

LIFESTYLE

TO AN OUTSIDER, HONG KONG'S endless crowds, traffic jams, skyscrapers, and rows of concrete apartment buildings may seem overwhelming, but Hong Kongers have learned to deal with life in one of the most densely populated places on earth.

Hong Kong was carved out of a rocky island by people with ambition, determination, and the desire to succeed economically. This motivation is reflected in Hong Kong's fiercely competitive business world. At the same time traditional Chinese values and customs play an important role in everyday life.

FAMILY

The family is the strongest social unit in Hong Kong. Children are taught that respecting their family and parents is their primary duty. This ensures that the family remains close knit.

In the old days the traditional family structure consisted of an extended family that lived together under one roof. However, given Hong Kong's space constraints, large families are no longer the norm. It is now common for children to move to their own apartments when they marry and begin to raise a family.

In the traditional family the man was the head of the household. His word was law. He went out to earn a living while his wife tended to the home and children. Now that more women are educated, working, and financially independent, conventional gender roles are changing. Women are challenging traditional thinking about their homebound status. The role of the household head is also changing. Children no longer accept the father's absolute authority. Today children often expect to have a say in family matters.

Above: **Boys take the plunge off a junk. Several thousand people live on boats around Hong Kong, but their numbers are dwindling.**

Opposite: **Locals shopping at the Central Market in Hong Kong.**

Grandparents are also affected by such social changes. In the traditional extended family grandparents were considered the keepers of wisdom, and their opinions were sought and respected. Because many members of the elder generation now live apart from their children and grandchildren, grandparents' influence on the family has decreased.

HOUSING

Housing has always been a problem in Hong Kong. It is estimated that over 40 percent of the territory's land area is unsuitable for development. As a result most Hong Kong residents live in high-rise apartments. Only the very wealthy reside on landed property. Many of these residences are mansions scattered in and around the southern hills of Hong Kong Island. Members of the middle class live at the base of the hills in cramped 1,000-square-foot (92-square-meter) apartments that cost an average of $1 million or more.

As Hong Kong developed and its population grew, housing costs rocketed out of the average resident's reach. Hundreds of thousands of people lived in squalid shantytowns. In 1953 a shantytown fire left 53,000 people homeless. The government's emergency relocation measures soon became a full-scale public housing program. Construction on a massive scale resulted in the creation of multistory apartment blocks that dot the landscape today. The apartment blocks are a vast improvement over the old shantytowns, but they are still terribly overcrowded.

High-rise apartments are clustered along the coast at Wah Fu.

FENG SHUI

Feng shui (fung soy), which means "wind and water," is a Chinese concept that is taken seriously by all Hong Kongers. Feng shui is about living in harmony with the natural environment and tapping the goodness of nature to ensure good fortune and health. All Hong Kong residents understand the importance of good feng shui. For them it is an essential ingredient for success.

Feng shui was first practiced in ancient China by farmers who believed that wind and water were important natural forces that had the power to either nurture or destroy their crops. The practice has developed into an art of positioning buildings and other structures, such as fountains, bridges, and graves, so that they exist in harmony with the surrounding environment. A specially designed compass measures the invisible forces that the Chinese believe exist beneath the earth. A balance of negative yin and positive yang forces in the immediate surroundings determines one's well-being.

Feng shui practitioners examine all aspects of a structure. When an existing building is involved, a feng shui master may suggest the best way to readjust the natural forces in order to create balance, perhaps by rearranging the furniture, repainting a room in a different color, or placing mirrors in front of doors to deflect negative energy. For a new building, a feng shui master's recommendations may range from site selection and building orientation to the alignment of doors and windows, as well as the placement of furniture.

The public housing program has a long-term strategy to produce new housing and to upgrade older estates to meet overwhelming demand. As land on Hong Kong Island and Kowloon becomes even scarcer and more expensive, new urban centers, known as new towns, have sprung up in outlying areas. Many people live on islands or in the New Territories and commute to work by ferry or train.

The Hong Kong Housing Authority (HKHA) and the Hong Kong Housing Society (HKHS) are responsible for the territory's accommodation program. Two billion dollars' worth of public expenditures was spent on housing in 2005 to 2006. The HKHA also finances the construction of schools, hospitals, and commercial buildings around the apartment blocks.

Hong Kong's public housing program offers a wide range of rental and home ownership systems.

RICH AND POOR

Hong Kong's wealthiest man is business tycoon Li Ka-shing. In 2007 Forbes *magazine estimated his fortune at $23 billion, which makes him the ninth richest man in the world.*

In Hong Kong there is a stark contrast between the lifestyles of the rich and poor. The very rich dwell in palatial homes and employ a bevy of cooks, gardeners, chauffeurs, and other domestic servants. Many of the rich are Chinese people who have made money as factory owners, bankers, or merchants. The neighborhood of choice for the wealthy is Victoria Peak, located high above the city with magnificent views of the harbor.

At the other end of the contrasting scale of lifestyles are homeless people who sleep under bridges or squatters who live in makeshift tents and cardboard homes at the edge of parks. Some of the older apartment blocks have deteriorated into virtual slums. However, the government has demolished the worst of these buildings and is constantly working to improve housing standards. A social security system is virtually nonexistent in Hong Kong.

The Hong Kong elite watch the horse races at Sha Tin Racecourse, located in Kowloon.

WORKING LIFE

The life of most Hong Kong residents is dominated by work and the pursuit of money. Hong Kong's commercial beginnings, combined with its emphasis on free trade, have focused people's attention on economic activities. The shortage of farming land, the influx of refugees determined to survive and prosper, and the lack of a social security system all contribute to an atmosphere in which work and profit are the highest priorities.

Vendors transporting their food in the Central Wet Market.

To ensure economic security for themselves and their families, people work long hours and often take extra jobs. Being one's own boss is highly valued. Small businesses have mushroomed, from fruit stalls to fortune-tellers and roadside barbers. Some families work from home, taking on simple but monotonous manufacturing jobs, such as assembling toy parts. There are laws that prevent children under the age of 14 from working in shops and factories, but in family businesses, even the children put in long hours to help the family survive.

On the streets of Hong Kong it seems as if everyone is always rushing to seal a business deal. Mobile phones are a common sight as people conduct business on the run. Peddlers, executives in suits, and millionaires in limousines all wield the latest communication gadgets. Everyone is out to make money.

Farmers and fishermen have a slower, quieter life, but they are still industrious. Women perform hard work in the fields, chatting with one another as they sift the soil and pull up weeds. Their lifestyle has barely changed in hundreds of years. However, many of the men in rural areas now work in industries around towns, leaving the women to tend the farms.

EDUCATION

Education is a central tenet of Confucianism. Hong Kongers see education as the key to a better life for their children and for themselves, since parents expect their children to look after them in their old age. As a result proper education is a priority. Children spend long hours studying at school and at home. Competition to get into the best high schools and universities is fierce.

About 90 percent of Hong Kong students attend government-aided schools. Until 1971 even public elementary schools charged fees, but the government now provides nine years of free compulsory education for pupils up to the age of 15. Chinese is the language of instruction in most schools. English is taught as a second language. Private English-language schools and international schools are open to children of all races.

After going through compulsory junior high school (grades 7–10), students take central examinations and are allocated places for grades 11 and 12, according to their test results. They may attend grammar, technical, or prevocational schools.

Full-time tertiary education in Hong Kong consists of one teacher-training college and seven universities, including the University of Hong Kong

The children of Causeway Bay enjoying an inline-skating excursion in Victoria Park.

Nine-year-old math whiz March Tian Boedihardjo became the youngest-ever student to attend college when he entered Hong Kong's Baptist University in 2007.

(which operates in the English language) and the Chinese University of Hong Kong (which operates in Chinese). Those students whose families can afford it may choose to study overseas, often in Britain, the United States, or Canada. Many Hong Kong parents send their children abroad in the hope that the children can obtain permanent residence in these countries. This would enable their families to leave Hong Kong if they ever decide to stop living under Chinese administration in the future.

Hong Kong also has more than 60 special schools for students with visual, hearing, physical, emotional, and mental disabilities. The Ministry of Education tries as much as possible to integrate children with disabilities into the mainstream school system.

Schoolgirls wait for the bus home. After a day at school, Hong Kong teenagers usually devote much of their time to studying.

WEDDINGS

The actual marriage ceremony, which often takes place at the registry of marriages, is usually a simple affair, with only close family members and friends in attendance. The traditional wedding banquet, however, is done on a much grander scale.

Wedding banquets in Hong Kong are a measure of one's status. The larger and more elaborate the banquet, the more "face" the bride and groom and their families will have. The result is a sit-down dinner for hundreds of people in a huge ballroom.

The other result of a huge wedding banquet is a huge bill. Traditionally the banquet is the financial responsibility of the groom's family, who treat the event as a celebration to welcome the future mother of their grandchildren. To help with the cost of the banquet, guests give *laisee* (ly-see)—red packets of lucky money—instead of gifts.

Wedding banquets are long, noisy affairs. The wedding meal usually has 10 courses, which means that dinner lasts for two to three hours. Then there are the obligatory speeches. In the course of the evening, the bride will change from a Western-style white wedding gown into a traditional red outfit. The wedding couple walks from

A happy couple poses for a shot after their wedding banquet. The bride is wearing traditional wedding clothes.

table to table to toast their guests and to receive lively toasts in return. When dessert is served the party draws to an end. The couple and their parents see their guests off at the doorway.

The most important part of the traditional wedding is the tea ceremony. The new bride serves tea to all of her in-laws who are older than her husband. Referred to as *zham cha* (tsum chah), which literally means "serve tea," the ceremony is a way for the bride to show her respect to the elders in her new family. In ancient times this practice was used to approve of the bride whom the groom had chosen. If his parents did not approve of the woman, they would not accept tea from the bride. Today family elders use the tea ceremony as an occasion to bestow their blessings on the couple.

FUNERALS

Like weddings, funerals in Hong Kong are an indicator of status. The more important and wealthy the deceased or the bereaved family is, the more people there will be at the funeral. When the funeral service begins the casket is wheeled into the funeral hall. Mourners are expected to walk around the casket to pay their last respects.

If the deceased person was Christian, a Christian funeral service follows. If he or she was Buddhist or Daoist, the family holds a wake that may last for several days, with a priest burning incense and chanting prayers. To ensure that the deceased has sufficient money and other luxury items in the afterlife, paper money and paper models of consumer goods, such as houses, cars, and even servants, are burned. It is believed that when these paper images burn, the smoke carries them up to the heavens.

This paper house is burned to provide the deceased with a good home in the afterlife.

This home for the elderly is run by the government and other charity organizations.

In 2005 life expectancy for Hong Kong males and females was estimated at 79 and 84.5 years, respectively. In 2033 men will probably live to be 82.5, while women will enjoy a longer lifespan of 88 years.

HEALTH CARE

Hong Kong residents enjoy good health due to extensive governmental implementation of community health services. The territory's low infant and maternal mortality rates are among the best in the world. Unfortunately Hong Kong's high population density means that it is occasionally susceptible to epidemics of major communicable diseases, such as avian flu and severe acute respiratory syndrome (SARS).

Hong Kong has government, government-assisted, and private hospitals. The Department of Health operates general outpatient clinics, as well as maternal and child health centers. Established in 1990 the Hospital Authority runs hospitals and specialized outpatient clinics. Mobile dispensaries serve villagers in remote areas of the New Territories, and islanders are visited by "floating clinics." Helicopters provide a "flying doctor" service to the more isolated and inaccessible communities.

Cases of tuberculosis, leprosy, and venereal disease are treated free of charge. Maternity and child health guidance, including

CONFUCIANISM

Hong Kongers view Confucian ethics as important concepts. These guiding principles were passed down by Confucius (551–479 B.C.), China's most famous and influential teacher and philosopher. Born at the time of the Warring States (403–221 B.C.), Confucius taught a system of moral statecraft that would lead to peace, stability, and a just government. He is venerated as the man who established the code of conduct that forms the basis for much of Chinese culture and lifestyle.

Confucianism is a system of ethical precepts for the management of society based on the practice of sympathy, or "human-heartedness," which is demonstrated through a combination of etiquette and ritual. Confucius set out a code of behavior for five categories of loyal relationships: the relationship of a subject to a ruler, a son to his father, a younger brother to an elder brother, a wife to her husband, and a friend to another friend. Respect and loyalty, integral parts of any relationship, are fundamental Confucian values that strengthen social harmony.

Filial piety—respect and obedience to one's family elders—is another important Confucian value. Filial piety is a cohesive force that binds families together, even in Westernized Hong Kong.

Medical staff give out free masks and pamphlets to the locals during the SARS outbreak.

prenatal services, postnatal care, and immunization, is also free. Free health-care services are available for children and adolescents at various stages of development. The elderly enjoy access to specialized health centers and medical care at little or no cost.

Despite the health-care system's successes, hospitals and clinics remain under great pressure, due to overcrowding. Patients often face a long wait for treatment.

SEVERE ACUTE RESPIRATORY SYNDROME (SARS)

In 2003 the outbreak of severe acute respiratory syndrome (SARS) brought Hong Kong to a standstill.

The epidemic started in Guangdong when several live-animal market workers died after being contaminated by the virus from civet cats. A doctor who had treated them traveled to Hong Kong, fell ill, and checked into a hospital. He died two weeks later, not knowing that he had infected a dozen guests who had been staying in the same hotel where he had stayed.

Only one of those people infected by the doctor was a Hong Kong resident. Within a week of that man's hospitalization, 50 health-care workers fell ill. Many of the doctors and nurses who were treating these patients also succumbed to the then-unidentified disease, and many of them died.

Meanwhile SARS was racing through other countries, as the infected hotel guests suffered high fevers upon returning home. People who had close contact with them were also stricken with the disease.

The World Health Organization (WHO) issued a global alert as SARS outbreaks were reported in Canada, Singapore, Taiwan, and Vietnam. Patients were often quarantined. The cause—a pathogen that was previously unknown in humans—was eventually discovered, and vaccines were developed. By then the disease had already provoked widespread panic and disrupted global travel.

SARS wrought damage far beyond its official death toll. The viral pandemic crippled Hong Kong psychologically, as entire communities and lifestyles grinded to a halt.

THE CONCEPT OF FACE

"Face" is an important concept in Chinese society. "Keeping face" means upholding a person's prestige in society. "Losing face" is avoided at all costs. A person could lose face by being ridiculed or reprimanded in public, which would result in a loss of prestige. "Giving face"—making sure not to inadvertently show someone up in public—is something that children learn from a young age.

RELIGION

MOST HONG KONG CHINESE PRACTICE a mix of Buddhism, Daoism, and Confucianism. Some people even combine these beliefs with Christianity. They go to church on Sunday and then visit a temple to burn joss sticks (incense sticks) for good luck. The practice of animism can still be found; offerings or joss sticks are placed at the foot of certain rocks and trees that are believed to house spirits. Hong Kongers are very tolerant of different religious beliefs.

Immigrants introduced Buddhism and Daoism to Hong Kong from mainland China. Some Buddhist and Daoist temples date back over seven centuries, while others were built in recent years with all the magnificence of traditional Chinese architecture. In all there are more than 600 Buddhist and Daoist temples in the territory. There are also almost 800 Christian churches and chapels, a handful of mosques, Hindu and Sikh temples, as well as a Jewish synagogue.

In the New Territories many villages retain traditional clan organizations. They have an ancestral hall where tablets inscribed with ancestors' names are kept and venerated. The hall is the center of both religious and secular activities among villagers.

Left: **Girls worshipping at the Daoist Wong Tai Sin Temple in Kowloon.**

Opposite: **Many devotees flock to Po Lin Temple to pay their respects to the huge Buddha statue.**

Prayers, candles, incense, and fruit are some of the offerings at Buddhist and Daoist temples.

BUDDHISM AND DAOISM

Prince Siddhartha Gautama founded Buddhism in India in the sixth century B.C. Disillusioned by the misery and injustice in the world Gautama renounced his royal heritage to seek enlightenment, which he attained after meditating for many years. After he became enlightened he was known as the Buddha. The term *Buddha* means "Enlightened One." The Buddha taught that the source of human suffering and misery springs from cravings and desires, and that meditating to eliminate desires can lead to spiritual enlightenment. Buddhism became established as a major religion in China in the sixth century A.D.

Daoism originated in China around 2,500 years ago. Its founder was Laozi, whose name means "Teacher" or "Old One." Daoism advocates a life of simplicity and passivity that follows the *dao* (*dow*, which rhymes with *how*)—the guiding path that leads to immortality. Many people who lived in harmony with nature, including Laozi, are now worshipped as Daoist gods.

Both Buddhism and Daoism were introduced to Hong Kong by Chinese immigrants, and the two religions' practices have merged to some extent. Almost every Buddhist and Daoist household has an ancestral shrine, and countless shops have a "God Shelf" that bears images of the owner's favorite deities. Traditional rites associated with birth, marriage, death, and festivals are still widely observed. Temples are especially crowded during festivals and on the first and 15th days of each lunar month. Although each temple is generally dedicated to one or occasionally two deities, it is common for the images of multiple deities to be displayed. Daoist priests perform elaborate rites, offering thanks to the gods or praying for prosperity and happiness.

Religious studies are conducted in monasteries, nunneries, and hermitages. Hong Kong's best-known monasteries are situated in more remote parts of the New Territories. The Buddhist Po Lin Monastery on Lantau Island is renowned for its view of the sunrise and its gigantic Buddha statue.

Daoist and Buddhist organizations provide grants to meet welfare, educational, and medical needs in Hong Kong, either directly or indirectly via donations to assorted charities.

The popular Man Mo Temple is run by a local charitable organization and is dedicated to the Gods of Literary Attainment and Martial Valor. The huge incense coils that hang from the ceiling are donated by pious worshippers.

TIN HAU, A GODDESS OF THE SEA

Hong Kong has always depended on the sea, first for fishing and then for trade. So it is not surprising that the territory's most popular deities are those associated with the sea and the weather. Tin Hau, the "Queen of Heaven" and protector of seafarers, is worshipped by an estimated 250,000 people. There are at least 24 Tin Hau temples in Hong Kong, with the earliest and most famous one at Fat Tong Mun in Joss House Bay.

CHRISTIANITY

Christianity in Hong Kong dates back almost to the founding of the territory. The first church was established in 1841. Today there are 52 Christian denominations and independent groups practicing in Hong Kong. The Christian community numbers around 660,000.

A Roman Catholic church was established in Hong Kong in 1841, and the territory became a diocese in 1946. In 1969 Francis Chen-peng Hsu became Hong Kong's first Chinese bishop. The present cardinal, Joseph Zen, succeeded his predecessor in 2002. There are about 240,000 Catholics in Hong Kong. Catholic services are usually conducted in Cantonese or Mandarin, with a few churches providing services in English.

One of the diocese's concerns is the community's well-being. As of 2005 the Catholic Board of Education has administered 313 Catholic schools and kindergartens. Catholic churches provide medical and social services through the running of hospitals, clinics, social centers, hostels, homes for the elderly, and a home for the handicapped. These services are open to people of all faiths, and it is estimated

Saint Francis Xavier Church.

that 95 percent of their beneficiaries are non-Catholics.

The Protestant community dates back to 1841. Baptists form the largest denomination, followed by Lutherans. Other major denominations include Adventists, Anglicans, and members of the Christian and Missionary Alliance, Church of Christ in China, Methodist, and Pentecostal churches. Due to their emphasis on youth work many congregations have a high proportion of young people. Since the 1970s the number of independent churches has increased significantly due to the evangelical zeal of lay Christians. Current membership numbers 320,000.

Protestant churches in Hong Kong are involved in education, health care, and social welfare. Protestant organizations operate three tertiary colleges and 630 schools that range from nursery school to secondary level. They also manage theological seminaries, Christian publishing houses, and bookshops. There are four Christian radio programs on Radio Television Hong Kong (RTHK). The Protestant movement also runs hospitals, clinics, and social service organizations. Their services include community and youth centers, day-care centers, children's homes, homes for the elderly, schools for the deaf, training centers for the mentally disabled, and camp sites.

A Catholic priest distributing Holy Communion during a church service.

A Chinese Muslim reads the Koran.

OTHER RELIGIONS

ISLAM There are approximately 90,000 Muslims in Hong Kong. About one-third of these are ethnic Chinese, while the rest hail from Pakistan, India, Malaysia, Indonesia, the Middle East, and Africa. There are three mosques on Hong Kong Island and one in Kowloon. The Shelley Street Masjid was the first to be built in Hong Kong, in the 1840s. The Kowloon Masjid and Islamic Center can accommodate about 2,000 worshippers.

The Incorporated Trustees of the Islamic Community Fund of Hong Kong—an organization consisting of the Islamic Union of Hong Kong, the Pakistan Association, the Indian Muslim Association, and the Dawoodi Bohra Association—coordinates all religious affairs, and manages mosques and Muslim cemeteries.

Charitable work among the Muslim community, such as financial aid to the needy, medical care, educational assistance, the provision of an Islamic kindergarten, and assistance for the aged, is conducted through various Muslim organizations in Hong Kong.

HINDUISM The religious and social activities of Hong Kong's strong Hindu community, which numbers 40,000, are centered around the Hindu Temple in Hong Kong Island's Happy Valley district. The Hindu Association of Hong Kong is responsible for the upkeep of the temple, which is used for the observance of Hindu festivals, meditation, spiritual lectures, yoga classes, devotional music sessions, and other community activities. Naming, engagement, and marriage ceremonies are performed at the temple according to Hindu rites. Other important services rendered by the temple include the administration of last rites, cremation ceremonies, and the upkeep of the Hindu crematorium at Cape Collinson.

The Khalsa Diwan temple serves the Sikh community in Hong Kong.

SIKHISM Hong Kong has a small Sikh community that numbers 8,000 members. Established in 1901, a unique feature of the Sikh Temple is that it provides free meals and short-term accommodation for overseas visitors of any faith.

JUDAISM Hong Kong's Jewish community worships at the Synagogue Ohel Leah, the Chabad Lubavitch, and several other locations. The synagogue was built in 1901 on land provided by Sir Jacob Sassoon and his family. The original site included a rabbi's residence and school, as well as a recreation club for the congregation of 1,000 members. A Jewish cemetery adjoins the synagogue. The main worship site once housed a school and club, which have since been redeveloped into two residential blocks of apartments. The new Jewish Community Center offers both recreational and kosher dining facilities. It also has a specialist library devoted to all aspects of Judaism.

LANGUAGE

THE ENGLISH AND CHINESE languages are both widely spoken in Hong Kong. Under the Official Languages Ordinance, enacted in 1974, both languages have equal status. Major reports and government publications are available in both English and Chinese versions. Simultaneous interpretation is provided at all government meetings. The civil service replies to correspondence from the public in either English or Chinese, depending on the language in which the initial correspondence is written. Since 1989 all new principal legislation is ratified in both languages.

China is a huge country, and over the centuries many distinct Chinese dialects have developed. A speaker of one dialect may not understand a speaker from a different part of China. Written Chinese, however, is the same for all dialects. The commonly spoken dialect in Hong Kong is Cantonese, which is Guangdong province's predominant dialect.

Left: **Many Chinese take their handwriting very seriously, as it is perceived as a reflection of their upbringing and character. Children spend hours practicing writing in order to develop and perfect a style that is easily decipherable yet graceful and aesthetically appealing to others.**

Opposite: **People reading the local newspapers during meal time.**

Friends gather in the park to converse and read newspapers together.

Prior to 1974 English was Hong Kong's only official language, and knowledge of English has always been key to employment in the civil service and multinational corporations. This situation began to change, however, after Hong Kong reverted to Chinese administration. The government is now encouraging more proficient use of Chinese in the civil service. The ultimate objective is to develop a civil service that is proficient in Cantonese, Putonghua (the official language of China, commonly known as Mandarin), and English.

Non-Cantonese Hong Kongers usually speak their own language or dialect among themselves. However, almost all the people who have been born and raised in Hong Kong can speak Cantonese, regardless of their race.

SPOKEN CHINESE

With well over a billion speakers worldwide, Chinese is the most widely spoken language in the world. However, it requires time for the non-

Chinese to grasp. The various tones are difficult to master, and the writing system is very complex.

Chinese has eight major dialects: Mandarin, Cantonese, Wu, Hakka (or *Kejia*), Xiang, Gan, northern Min, and southern Min.

Although Cantonese originated in China's Guangdong province, Hong Kong's people have their own distinctive style of speech. Cantonese is the language of the streets, and it is also the prime language of Hong Kong's popular culture. Almost all of the territory's movies and songs are produced and performed in Cantonese.

In China, Mandarin is spoken by at least 70 percent of the Han people, who constitute more than 90 percent of the total population. The official language of China is based on the Mandarin that is spoken in Beijing and is known as Putonghua or "common speech." References

LEARN TO COUNT IN CANTONESE:

one – *yat*
two – *yih*
three – *sam*
four – *sei*
five – *ngh*
six – *luk*
seven – *chat*
eight – *baat*
nine – *gau*
ten – *sahp*

COMMON CANTONESE EXPRESSIONS

Zhang (tseng) means "cool," "neat," "fine," or "excellent." It can apply to situations, people, or objects. You can have *zhang* cars, *zhang* clothes, and *zhang* books. When applied to people, it means that they are physically attractive. *Ho zhang wo* adds emphasis—meaning "really cool" or "excellent."

Yau mo gau cho (yow mo gow cho) literally means "Has something gotten messed up?" but can be interpreted as "Are you kidding me?" It is a good phrase to use when you are frustrated that things are not going your way.

Lei po (lay poh) means "ridiculous". If you are really frustrated with the situation, you can say *lei sai po* (lay sy poh).

to standard Chinese or simply to Chinese usually mean Putonghua.

Chinese is a tonal language. This means that the same syllable can have different meanings depending on the way it is pronounced. For example, by speaking in different tones (such as rising, falling, high, or low), the syllable *ma* in Putonghua can mean "mother," "hemp," "horse," or "scold." Putonghua has four distinct tones, whereas Cantonese has nine.

Both Chinese and Cantonese have an abundance of homonyms—words that sound the same but have different meanings—for example, *meet* and *meat*. In Hong Kong, when a word sounds like something auspicious, it takes on a special significance. The word for "bat" is *fu*, which sounds like the word *fu*, meaning "good luck." Fish (*yu*) sounds like "plenty" (*yu*). As a result bats and fish are considered lucky creatures, and they are featured in all sorts of designs and decorations. On the other hand the number four (*sei*) is considered unlucky because it sounds like the word for "death" in Cantonese.

WRITTEN CHINESE

Although spoken Chinese dialects may differ enormously, all literate Chinese speakers can

DEALING WITH ENGLISH AND PUTONGHUA

Even though most high school students in Hong Kong study English as a first or second language, the general standard of spoken English is poor. Most Hong Kong Chinese think of English as a foreign language, and very few communicate in English outside the classroom. However, mastery of English is still viewed as an essential step toward getting a good job or emigrating. This translates into a reasonably high demand for English-language schools. There are also language schools that teach conversational English to adults who wish to improve their job prospects.

Many Hong Kong emigrants who have settled in English-speaking environments around the world will quickly realize that the English they learned in school is really a mix of English and Cantonese that is not very useful outside of Hong Kong. Many end up hiring a private tutor to help them communicate in their new place of residence.

Today Hong Kong residents have to learn Putonghua, the official language of China, in addition to English. Although the writing system is the same for Cantonese and Putonghua, the spoken language is completely different. Learning to speak it is supposedly as difficult as learning English. Putonghua is currently taught from the first year of primary school until the last year of secondary school.

Opposite: **Whereas English letters spell out the sounds of a word, a single Chinese character represents a complete idea (in this case, the idea of "full").**

Hong Kong is one of the most wired communities in Asia. In 2005 almost 5 million Hong Kongers were registered Internet users.

communicate with one another in writing, because all Chinese characters are written the same way, regardless of dialect. This makes it easier for the Chinese government to disseminate information about policies in Hong Kong. The government is able to reach Cantonese-speaking Hong Kongers in writing.

Written Chinese is based on ideograms. This means that each character is frequently a pictorial representation of an idea. For example, the Chinese character for "mountain" is represented by a simplified line drawing of a mountain. In the early stages of the language one ideogram represented one word. As more words were gradually added to the language, two or more elements were combined to form a new ideogram. Sometimes two ideograms represent one idea. There are more than 50,000 characters in written Chinese. Of these, about 3,000 are in common use. The simplest character has only one stroke, while the most complicated has 30. Not surprisingly it is common for Chinese speakers to consult a dictionary to look up characters they have not seen before or those that they have forgotten how to write.

The Chinese government introduced a simplified form of Chinese characters in 1964, because it believed that the writing system was too complicated for the average person. The simplified characters retain the basic shape and meaning of the original characters, but they have fewer strokes. In Hong Kong, however, the traditional form of written characters has been retained.

TELEVISION

Hong Kong has four local television channels that command a total daily audience of almost six million people. This means that nearly every resident of Hong Kong watches television daily. The main broadcasters

are Television Broadcasts Ltd (TVB) and Asia Television Ltd (ATV). Both provide separate Chinese- and English-language services.

Satellite television first came to Hong Kong in 1991, when Star TV was broadcast to the entire Asian region. Star TV provides sports, music, news, and Hindi and Chinese programs. Cable television was introduced to Hong Kong only in 1993, when Wharf Cable launched its service with an initial eight channels. By 1995 it had expanded to 20 channels, including four

Hong Kong's singer and actress Miriam Yeung performs during the Grand Variety Show, celebrating the anniversary of China's and Hong Kong's reunification.

Literally hundreds of magazines are available in Hong Kong.

pay-per-view movie channels. As of 2003, 130 pay television channels were available to 860,000 subscribers.

NEWSPAPERS AND MAGAZINES

At the last count about 800 publications were registered in Hong Kong. At least 10 percent are newspapers, including Chinese-language dailies, English dailies, bilingual titles, and other language papers.

The Chinese-language dailies cover general news, both local and overseas. Top-selling papers include *Ming Pao*, *Apple Daily*, and *Oriental*

Daily. The last two specialize in entertainment, especially television and movie updates and horse racing. The larger papers are distributed to Chinese communities overseas.

Periodicals also enjoy a booming business in Hong Kong. More than 600 publications are registered, over half of which are in Chinese. The numerous titles cover an extensive range of subjects, from current affairs to technical knowledge and entertainment guides.

Hong Kong is the Southeast Asian base of operations for many global and regional media. International news agencies such as the Associated Press are represented in the territory. International papers such as the *Asian Wall Street Journal* and the *International Herald Tribune* have locally printed editions, as do international current affairs magazines such as *Newsweek*. Regional magazines including *Asiaweek* and the *Far Eastern Economic Review* are also based in Hong Kong.

The South China Morning Post *is Hong Kong's highest-circulating English-language newspaper.*

FREEDOM OF THE PRESS

Despite the Basic Law's guarantee of "freedom of speech, of the press, and of publication," Hong Kong's media scene has been increasingly pressurized into self-censorship. The People's Republic of China has a poor record when it comes to free speech. The media are not permitted to criticize the Communist Party, and journalists may be convicted of espionage and jailed for long periods, even for life, if they do not follow the government's line. The official Chinese news agency, Xinhua, has the right to censor news. Hong Kong's huge media industry, which is said to be the freest in Asia, is struggling to maintain objective coverage in the face of economic and political constraints.

ARTS

HONG KONG HAS A lively arts scene. Every year Hong Kong residents can enjoy hundreds of cultural events, from traditional Chinese opera, puppet shows, and classical music performances to Western ballet and theater. The Hong Kong Philharmonic Orchestra, the Hong Kong Chinese Orchestra, the Chung Ying Theater Company, and the City Contemporary Dance Company are among the best-known local artistic groups. Art exhibitions showcase the works of local and international painters and sculptors. Hong Kong is a major center for the sale of Asian art and antiques. Hollywood Road in the Central District is crowded with antique and curio shops, while major auction houses such as Sotheby's and Christie's have offices in Hong Kong. The territory's entertainment industry is world renowned. Cantonese movies and music are increasingly exported beyond Asia to the rest of the world.

Left: **The Hong Kong Cultural Center, which is located on the tip of the Kowloon peninsula.**

Opposite: **A Chinese opera performer painting her face before a show.**

CALLIGRAPHY

The Chinese have developed calligraphy into an art form. In earlier centuries scholars had to master calligraphy in order to pass the all-important civil service examination, and great importance is still placed on good handwriting.

All that an artist requires for Chinese calligraphy is a brush, an ink stick, an ink stone, and paper. Calligraphers write poems, couplets, or proverbs. A well-written calligraphic piece plays on the senses, with the brush strokes invoking images of strength, beauty, or grace. Even if one cannot interpret what the characters mean, the piece still is appreciated for its aesthetic value.

Right: **Chinese calligraphy requires both physical and mental control.**

Opposite: **An artist painting colorful flowers onto a folding paper fan.**

There are several forms of calligraphy. The formal style has angular characters and few curved lines. Characters written in the "grass" style are more flowing and cursive. Only those who have studied Chinese calligraphy intensively can decipher characters that are written in this style.

PAINTING

Chinese paintings are usually done on silk or absorbent paper. There are five categories of subjects: human figures, landscapes, flowers, birds and other animals, and fish and insects. A pointed brush is used for coloring. Some styles only use black paint, while others are more colorful.

Chinese artists do not paint with a model before them. They paint from the images in their memory. Their work is swift, and the brush strokes are confident. Once done the artist may paint the picture many times over until he or she achieves the desired effect. Chinese artists do not simply paint an image; they also attempt to capture the spirit in their creation. To that end artists sometimes spend hours meditating and concentrating before expressing their thoughts on the paper. Many artists are known to paint only certain subjects, such as horses or birds.

Painted porcelain for sale in an antique shop on Hollywood Road.

Artists are evaluated on their brush strokes. Brush strokes are given special names, and critics examine how the brush strokes contribute to the effect of the picture. Calligraphy in the form of a couplet or a short stanza of poetry is almost always used to complete a painting, as it is believed to complement the picture.

FINE ARTS

The Chinese are well known for their porcelain and ceramic artifacts. Vases, urns, bowls, and plates are adorned with symbols of nature, the seasons, or myths. Sometimes they are decorated with calligraphy. The best known is the Ming style of blue-and-white porcelain.

Cloisonné is another popular fine art. Cloisonné is a method of decorating metal surfaces with enamel. Metal pieces are attached to a base plate, forming sections that are filled in with enamel paint. When the piece is heated the enamel fuses to the metal, forming a glossy, colored surface.

Although the art was introduced to China from the Middle East, the Chinese perfected the technique. Today cloisonné decorates everything from chairs to chopsticks.

The Chinese are also masters of carving. Jade, ivory, and rosewood are intricately carved. Sometimes knives as small as toothpicks are used for finer work. Carved rosewood furniture inlaid with intricate mother-of-pearl designs are popular items.

CHINESE OPERA

Chinese opera started out as street performances where gongs, cymbals, and drums were used to attract passersby. Even today a piece with these instruments would herald the beginning of a new opera scene. Opera plots are taken from historical tracts, folk legends, classical novels, and fairy tales. Opera includes a combination of many skills, such as singing, dramatic speech, acrobatics, and dancing. An orchestra of Chinese fiddles, flutes, clappers, drums, cymbals, and gongs usually complements the action.

Chinese opera stages are usually quite bare and have few props. Chairs may represent hills. A flag with the character for "river" written on it represents a body of water. However, the lack of scenery is more than made up for by the intricately embroidered costumes and glittery headgear that the performers wear. Artists wear robes with long, wide sleeves. The sleeves are used for flirting and for depicting fear or anger. The actors' makeup is very heavy

Chinese opera performers use dramatic gestures and high-pitched falsetto. Perfecting this vocal style requires years of dedicated practice.

97

and elaborate, with different colors signifying different character traits, such as loyalty or intelligence. Gods and fairies are represented with gold or silver makeup. Yellow is the color of emperors, and green represents a person of high rank.

Operas usually last for several hours. The atmosphere is festive, and the action is not limited to the actors on stage. Spectators stand up and join in the chorus. Their loud comments in response to the stage action are often as entertaining as the opera itself. Sadly this art form is declining, as young Hong Kongers increasingly favor entertainment alternatives from the West.

An ensemble of traditional Chinese instruments.

CHINESE ORCHESTRAS

Traditional Chinese music is popular with Hong Kong's older population. The 85-member Chinese Orchestra holds regular concerts at the Cultural Center and in other halls throughout the territory.

Traditional musical instruments include the *erhu* (ER-hoo), a two-stringed fiddle; the *yue chin* (YOO-eh chin), a four-stringed banjo; the *guzheng* (KOO-chuhng), zither; the *hu chin* (HOO chin), a two-stringed violin; and the *pipa* (PEE-pah), a four-stringed lute.

For the uninitiated traditional Chinese music may be difficult to appreciate. In order to appeal to a wider range of tastes, including Western audiences, the traditional instruments are being modified, or accompanied by Western instruments such as the cello, and are being used experimentally to perform modern compositions.

CANTOPOP

Hong Kong is the center of a thriving Cantonese pop music industry, commonly called "Cantopop." It is based on Western popular musical forms, rather than traditional Chinese music.

Cantopop stars have a huge following in Hong Kong, Taiwan, Singapore, and other Chinese-speaking communities. They also have many fans in Asian countries such as Japan. They are even popular among people who do not speak Cantonese. Many of the singers record songs in Putonghua, and some even record in Japanese.

Among the biggest Cantopop stars are four solo male singers whose popularity has earned them the title of "Heavenly Kings"—Andy Lau, Aaron Kwok, Jacky Cheung, and Leon Lai. Major female stars include Faye Wong, Sandy Lam, and the pop duo Twins. Although these singers are virtually unknown outside of Asia, top performers (such as Jacky Cheung) often sell as many records as Michael Jackson or Madonna. Their publicity tours attract legions of loyal fans who range from prepubescent teens to working adults and retirees.

The four "Heavenly Kings" of Hong Kong's popular music (*left to right*): Andy Lau, Aaron Kwok, Leon Lai, and Jacky Cheung. The hairstyles, dress, and mannerisms of the big Cantopop stars are often widely imitated.

Jackie Chan during the premiere of his movie *Shanghai Knights*.

MOVIES

Hong Kong is the world's largest producer of Chinese-language action movies. The territory also exports movies all over Asia, even to non-Chinese-speaking countries. These days Hong Kong movies have gained a following in the United States. Many Hong Kong stars are now household names around the world. Here are some of them:

JACKIE CHAN is the reigning king of action cinema, thanks to his comedy/martial arts movies. Having starred in the *Rush Hour* series, he is a familiar face to American audiences. Recently Chan received an MTV lifetime achievement award.

CHOW YUN-FAT is one of Hong Kong's most prolific actors. Chow has acted in movies of every genre and was one of the stars in the internationally acclaimed *Crouching Tiger, Hidden Dragon*, directed by Academy Award–winning director Ang Lee.

BRUCE LEE, born Lee Sui Lung, remains a movie legend. He was probably the first Chinese martial arts actor to become a well-known figure in the West and a household name around Asia. His son Brandon followed in his footsteps. They both died mysteriously at a young age.

JOHN WOO earned himself a place in film history by directing many Hong Kong action movies. He grabbed Hollywood's attention with films such as *Broken Arrow* and 1997's *Face Off* starring John Travolta and Nicolas Cage. His best-known works—*The Killer, Bullet in the Head,* and *Hard Boiled*—show characters struggling with questions of loyalty and honor. Woo's distinctive style is conveyed through elaborately choreographed action sequences. Film festivals, independent movie theaters, videotapes, and laser disks have earned him a legion of new fans.

Women in Hong Kong cinema are not relegated to soft roles. They are often central characters in kung fu or martial arts movies, wielding swords, performing acrobatics, and felling bad guys with the best of the men. Some of the better-known Hong Kong actresses are Maggie Cheung, Anita Mui, and Anita Yuen.

Bruce Lee in action prior to his mysterious death.

THE SHAW BROTHERS

There are several Shaw brothers in the entertainment industry, but the best known are Runme Shaw and Sir Runrun Shaw. They began Hong Kong's oldest film studio, thereby setting in motion an industry that turned Hong Kong into Asia's Hollywood.

Sir Runrun was a pioneer in Hong Kong filmmaking, producing Hong Kong's first movie with sound. The Shaw brothers' studios became the hub of the film industry during the 1960s and 1970s. Many great action stars and directors began their craft at the studio, which was one of the largest and most advanced in Asia at the time. The Shaw movie empire exported its films to other countries in Asia and successfully branched out into movie distribution and exhibition.

1.20M

LEISURE

THE PEOPLE OF HONG KONG do not have much time to spend on leisure, because they are busy working during the week. Most leisure activities are confined to weekends. Workdays are long, with offices opening at 8:30 A.M. Most people leave work between 6:00 and 7:00 P.M. Then there is the long commute back home, which may take an hour or more, depending on where workers live. Schoolchildren do not have much leisure time either. They are kept busy with homework and studies after school is over.

On weekends, however, Hong Kongers enjoy themselves thoroughly. Families picnic in the park, visit the outlying islands, take a trip to the amusement park, or swim and tan themselves at the beach. Weekends are also a time for the family to dine out and perhaps indulge in special dishes that are too time-consuming to prepare at home. Movie theaters have local and foreign movies that cater to all tastes.

Those who prefer more active forms of leisure engage in different forms of sports, including golf, cricket, soccer, tennis, and squash. The Urban Council and other government organizations provide courts and sports grounds. The wealthy enjoy pleasure boating, sailing, and waterskiing in Hong Kong's many inlets and bays.

The elderly, who have more leisure time, may spend time playing board games. The two most popular board games are Chinese chess and *weiqi* (way-chee). Mah-jongg, a game played with tiles, is also phenomenally popular. This is partly because it involves gambling, and for many Hong Kongers, gambling is a passion.

Above: **Expatriates enjoy a day out on a pleasure boat.**

Opposite: **Locals enjoy a leisurely swim at an indoor swimming pool.**

GOVERNMENT LEISURE PROGRAMS

In recent years the people of Hong Kong have been able to pursue a variety of recreational activities in their leisure time. Government programs to provide sports and other recreational facilities continue to expand each year, and thousands of events attract enthusiastic participants and supporters.

Sporting activities are coordinated by organizations such as the Urban Council, the Regional Council, the Home Affairs Department,

The 60-mile (100-km) "Trailwalker" charity walk is a popular annual event.

the Hong Kong Sports Institute, the Hong Kong Sports Development Board, and many voluntary associations. These organizations operate indoor games halls, soccer pitches, roller-skating rinks, jogging tracks, tennis courts, basketball courts, volleyball courts, squash courts, badminton courts, hockey fields, rugby grounds, outdoor and indoor stadiums, children's playgrounds, camping grounds, beaches, swimming pool complexes, parks and gardens, aviaries, and a zoo. They also provide indoor recreational facilities, such as art and craft rooms.

PARK OUTINGS

Contrary to the popular belief that Hong Kong is nothing more than a concrete cityscape, the territory actually has many parks scattered throughout its various regions. Its country park system covers 40 percent of the total land area.

Parks are important venues for leisure activities. Almost every day parks are full of people walking, exercising, or just relaxing. On weekdays parks are busiest in the early morning. This is when the young and old visit the park to exercise before going to work or school. Groups of people practice martial arts; children play games such as badminton; older men sit under the trees playing Chinese chess.

A man relaxing with his chihuahuas in a park.

On Sundays parks are often converted into fair sites. The streets are cordoned off, crowds gather around the ice cream and soda stalls, and people from all walks of life enjoy free performances. Parks in more remote areas are ideal spots for kite flying, picnicking, hiking, cycling, and camping.

An instructor leads a tai chi class. Tai chi can be practiced with or without implements such as swords and fans.

TAI CHI

Every morning Hong Kong is filled with people practicing tai chi. This Chinese martial art is primarily practiced for health. Tai chi emphasizes complete relaxation and is essentially a form of meditation; hence its nickname, "meditation in motion." Unlike conventional martial arts, tai chi is characterized by gentle, slow, flowing movements, which are precisely executed. Each action emphasizes force, rather than brute strength.

Tai chi traces its roots back to yoga, which was introduced to China from India. It gradually evolved into a Chinese martial art. In the 13th century a Daoist monk adapted the martial art into what has come to be known as tai chi. Over the centuries different styles evolved. The Yang style is the most common traditional form of tai chi practiced today.

The *chi* in the term *tai chi* refers to an ancient Chinese concept of energy. This energy, or chi, flows throughout the body, but it can become blocked, causing the body to become ill. There are several means of releasing the flow of chi. Two of the more commonly known methods are acupuncture and tai chi.

In addition to its physical benefits, tai chi is believed to bring about certain psychological effects. As a form of meditation it can help people understand themselves and enable them to deal with others more effectively. Tai chi is based on the Daoist belief that there are two opposing principles in the universe: yin and yang. By restoring the balance of yin and yang through tai chi, people can improve their physical and spiritual well-being.

Although tai chi used to be practiced mainly by the elderly, it has now caught on with the younger generation, who view it as a means of relieving stress.

The slow, meditative movements of tai chi give a sense of harmony to this scene.

LEE LAI SHAN, OLYMPIC CHAMPION

Although Hong Kong has been sending athletes to the Olympic Games since 1952, the territory only entered the medal tally for the first time in 1996, when windsurfer Lee Lai Shan struck gold at the Atlanta games. A native of Cheung Chau Island, Lee is now a hero in Hong Kong. Hundreds of people crowded the airport to welcome her home, and thousands more lined the route of her motorcade upon her triumphant return. When she arrived on the island she found that the inhabitants had covered the planks of the wooden jetty with a huge red carpet. She was welcomed with numerous streamers and banners, as well as a lion dance and a band.

Ocean Park's Water World is known for being Asia's largest water park.

BEACHES, POOLS, AND OCEAN PARK

When the scorching summer heat strikes swimming becomes Hong Kongers' recreation of choice. The government has designated 43 beaches as safe spots for aquatic activities. However, beaches where sharks have been spotted are off limits. There are also 27 public swimming pool complexes throughout Hong Kong Island, Kowloon, and the New Territories. Four of these are heated pools for winter use.

A must-visit vacation spot for both kids and adults is Ocean Park Hong Kong, also called Ocean Park. Located in Aberdeen on Hong Kong Island, it combines both an oceanarium and amusement park facilities. A range of rides, such as Ferris wheels and roller coasters, is available. Ocean Park also boasts the educational Dinosaur Discovery Trail, the Goldfish Pagoda, and the Butterfly House. Other attractions include a 738-foot (225-m) outdoor escalator, two aviaries, a bird theater, and a cultural village that teaches children about Chinese history, arts, crafts, mythology, customs, and inventions.

NIGHTLIFE

Hong Kong is famous for its nightlife. Bars, nightclubs, pubs, and restaurants populate Kowloon's Tsim Sha Tsui and Wanchai on Hong Kong Island. There are also dozens of hostess bars and Chinese ballrooms. Some of these establishments are very expensive and cater mainly to big-spending tourists, sailors on shore leave, and foreign businessmen. However, less flamboyant options abound. Clubs offer a range of live music, including jazz, blues, and rock. For night owls numerous discos beckon with bright neon signs. Imports such as Planet Hollywood, the Hard Rock Café, and British-style pubs are becoming increasingly popular among young people.

A popular nightlife spot is the karaoke bar. *Karaoke* (ka-ra-OH-kay) is a Japanese word that means "empty orchestra." People sing along to music videos that feature instrumental versions of popular songs. The lyrics are shown on the screen, and the karaoke singer warbles along. Part of the fun—or torture—lies in hearing someone mangling your favorite tune in public. Whether the singer is good or not, karaoke is an unforgettable experience. It has proven to be so popular that many bars and nightclubs now offer it.

Karaoke clubs provide private rooms with television sets, karaoke videos, and a microphone. Groups of friends can rent one of the private rooms to enjoy a sing-along.

A group of friends absorbed in their game of mah-jongg.

MAH-JONGG

Mah-jongg, an ancient Chinese game with many variations, is probably the number-one pastime in Hong Kong. A mah-jongg set of tiles is something like a deck of cards. There are 152 tiles, of which 108 are suit tiles (there are three suits). The rest are symbols and are generally more valuable than the suit tiles. The object of the game is to build sets of tiles.

Mah-jongg is a very lively game, with much clattering of tiles and friendly conversation. Four people are needed to play the game. The tiles are turned over and mixed up, or "washed." Each player then chooses a certain number of tiles. The players take turns to discard and pick up new tiles. The first player to build a complete set wins. There are very complicated rules governing how the sets can be built. Different types of sets command different points. The game can be played with or without gambling. Gambling comes in when the players agree on how much each point is worth before the game commences.

BOARD GAMES

In parks or in the common areas of public housing estates, one usually finds men seated on stools bending over board games. These men are playing either Chinese chess or *weiqi* (also known as *go*), games that require a great deal of strategy.

Chinese chess traces its roots back to the eighth century. Chess pieces include elephants, cavalry, infantry, and a fortress where the king and his counselors are entrenched. The two halves of the board are separated by the Yellow River. The objective is to storm the opponent's fortress and capture the military commanders.

A horse race under way at Happy Valley.

Weiqi has been around for thousands of years, and is the oldest board game in China. It is played on a grid of 19 horizontal and 19 vertical lines. The pieces consist of 181 black and 180 white flat, round counters. The object of the game is to capture the opponent's counters and territory. Because of the high number of possible moves, *weiqi* is considered the most complicated board game in the world.

HORSE RACING

Scores of Hong Kong Chinese love to gamble on horse races. When the races are under way at Happy Valley, many people take leave from work to attend, hoping to strike it rich. Hong Kong residents take note of race times and dates so that they know when to avoid the masses of traffic that head to and from the racetrack.

Horse racing is organized by the Hong Kong Jockey Club, which also operates lotteries.

FESTIVALS

THE MAJOR FESTIVALS IN HONG KONG follow the Chinese calendar. The Gregorian calendar followed in the West is a solar calendar that is based on the movements of the sun. The ancient Chinese calendar, however, is lunar (based on the moon). The starting dates of each month vary from year to year, according to the phases of the moon.

The Lunar New Year is the most important festival in Hong Kong. Other important Chinese celebrations include the Ching Ming Festival in the spring, the Dragon Boat Festival in early summer, the Festival of Hungry Ghosts, and the Mid-Autumn Festival. These events are thousands of years old and are celebrated by Chinese people all over the world.

Opposite: **Cherry blossoms and mini- mandarin plants are commonly sighted during Chinese New Year.**

THE CHINESE ZODIAC

The Chinese calendar moves in a 12-year cycle. Each year is dedicated to an animal. According to legend the Buddha summoned all the animals of the kingdom when he was dying. The first 12 to arrive had years assigned to them. People born under each sign are said to possess certain characteristics.

Rat (1972, 1984, 1996, 2008) — Charming, smart, creative, thrifty
Ox (1973, 1985, 1997, 2009) — Steadfast, methodical, reliable
Tiger (1974, 1986, 1998, 2010) — Dynamic, warm, sincere
Rabbit (1975, 1987, 1999, 2011) — Humble, artistic, clear-sighted
Dragon (1976, 1988, 2000, 2012) — Flamboyant, imaginative, lucky
Snake (1977, 1989, 2001, 2013) — Discreet, sensual, refined, intelligent
Horse (1978, 1990, 2002, 2014) — Sociable, competitive, adamant
Sheep (1979, 1991, 2003, 2015) — Artistic, fastidious, weak-willed
Monkey (1980, 1992, 2004, 2016) — Witty, popular, versatile, good-humored
Rooster (1981, 1993, 2005, 2017) — Aggressive, alert, perfectionistic
Dog (1982, 1994, 2006, 2018) — Honest, traditional, sympathetic
Pig (1983, 1995, 2007, 2019) — Caring, diligent, home loving

Dragon dance being performed for New Year.

Most businesses close during the three public holidays of the Chinese New Year, and a few close for longer. About a week before the New Year, barbers and hairdressers charge double their usual prices, since almost everyone needs a haircut to look good for the New Year!

CHINESE NEW YEAR

The first day of the first lunar month is the Chinese New Year, the most important festival for Hong Kong Chinese. It falls in late January or February. Because it marks the start of the year, every care is taken to ensure good fortune for the coming 12 months. Buildings are decorated and streets are strung with elaborate light displays. A huge fireworks display is held over Victoria Harbor, usually on the second day of the festival. Lion dances and other celebrations can be seen at hotels and in various residential areas.

Preparations usually begin with a thorough spring-cleaning. The home is decorated with good-luck symbols, such as bushes laden with tiny oranges (kumquats)—the Chinese word for "kumquats" sounds like the words for "gold" and "luck." People buy new clothes, fill rice bins and larders to the brim, mend quarrels, and repay debts.

The reunion dinner on New Year's Eve is significant. No matter how far from home people are, many travel back to dine with their parents. After all, the family that eats together stays together. Certain preparations are traditional: raw fish symbolizes prosperity, while the New Year's cake made from rice flour represents unity. At midnight all the house lights are turned on to dispel bad luck that may be lurking in dark corners. Crowds pack the temples to offer prayers for prosperity in the coming year.

On New Year's Day everyone dresses up in new clothes to visit relatives and friends, and children receive *laisee.* People greet one another by saying *kung hay fat choy,* which means "wishing you prosperity." On this day, no work—not even housework—is done, in case good luck might be inadvertently chased away. Use of knives and scissors is avoided. Even falling down is considered a bad omen.

In some villages of the New Territories lanterns are hung in ancestral halls during the Chinese New Year. Any local family that had a son born during the past year brings a lantern to the hall, and the men of the family gather to enjoy a special meal. It is a time of community-wide celebration.

An elderly lady is choosing lucky charms to decorate the house. The colors considered most auspicious are red and gold.

THE KITCHEN GOD'S DAY

On the day before the Lunar New Year the Kitchen God judges the family's behavior and travels to heaven to make a report to the Jade Emperor. The picture of the Kitchen God is taken down and ceremonially burned outside the kitchen to send him on his way. Before he leaves he is worshipped with incense and candles. He is served a delicious meal of glutinous rice, honey, or sugar, and sometimes wine as well. These foods are smeared all over his mouth to make sure that what he says will be sweet and flattering.

Offerings are made to the Goddess of the Sea during the Tin Hau festival.

MOONCAKES

Mooncakes (pastries filled with sweet, mashed lotus paste) are synonymous with the Mid-Autumn Festival. Besides symbolizing goodwill these small pastries were also responsible for ending the Mongol-controlled Yuan Dynasty (1271–1368). Chinese rebels stuffed each mooncake with a note informing supporters about their rebellion date—the 15th day of the eighth lunar month.

FESTIVAL OF TIN HAU

Tin Hau, Queen of Heaven and Goddess of the Sea, enjoys a soft spot in the Hong Konger's heart. Legend has it that Tin Hau was once a mortal. She was born long ago on the 23rd day of the third lunar month. Shortly before her birth a red light was seen descending upon the house of her father (who was a poor fisherman).

One day Tin Hau dreamed of her father and two brothers on their fishing junks in a storm. In her dream she grabbed the rigging and started to pull them ashore. At that moment her mother woke Tin Hau, causing her to let go of one of the ropes. When her brothers returned they told how a beautiful girl had walked across the raging waters and had dragged their junk to safety but said that she had been unable to save their father.

After Tin Hau's death sailors began to tell stories of her appearing during storms and rescuing them from certain death. The red light that appeared at the time of her birth was seen upon masts. Viewed as a sign of Tin Hau's protection, it was called "Our Mother's Fire."

Today almost every Hong Kong ship carries her image, and dozens of temples in Hong Kong are dedicated to her. On her birthday fishermen decorate their boats and gather at her temples to pray for good catches during the coming year.

CHING MING

In April, on the 106th day after the winter solstice, families visit cemeteries to sweep their ancestors' graves, repaint the inscriptions on the headstones, and show their respect. This festival is called *Ching Ming*, which means "Clear and Bright." Incense sticks and red candles are lit. Rice, wine, tea, and other foods are set out, and paper clothing and spirit money are burned. The whole family kneels to pay their respects. Before they leave they tuck several pieces of offering paper under a stone on top of the grave. This is a sign that the grave has been tended for another year.

Despite its solemn origins Ching Ming rites have the atmosphere of a picnic because the family members eat the food offerings. The festival is a happy occasion when families get together to remember their ancestors.

THE BUN FESTIVAL

The Bun Festival, unique to Hong Kong takes place on Cheung Chau usually in May. The central attractions are three 60-foot (18-m) towers studded with pink and white buns. The buns are an offering to the ghosts of the islanders who, according to stories, were killed by a plague or by pirates.

During the four days of celebration religious observances, processions, and Chinese opera performances take place. On the third day people dressed in colorful costumes march, walk on stilts, or ride on floats through

A lion dance at the Bun Festival, with the towers of Buns behind. At the climax of the festival, the crowds used to scramble up the towers to claim buns for good luck. After fights broke out and a tower collapsed, the scramble was abandoned.

the winding streets of the village. At the end of the festival, after the ghosts have had their fill, the buns are distributed to the crowds.

THE DRAGON BOAT FESTIVAL

The Dragon Boat Festival in the fifth lunar month combines a traditional celebration with the exciting pace of a sporting event.

It originated with the story of Wat Yuen, a famous poet and royal minister who threw himself into a river when his king fell under the influence of corrupt officials and refused to heed Wat Yuen's wise advice. When the people realized that Wat Yuen had drowned they threw rice into the water, hoping that the fish would eat the rice and spare his body. The dragon boats race every year as if they are looking for Wat Yuen's body, and everybody eats dumplings filled with meat and sticky rice wrapped in leaves.

The rowers sit two abreast in the long, narrow body of the dragon. The boats' heads and tails are dismantled and kept in local temples when they are not in use. New heads must be dedicated in a ceremony that involves painting each eye with a dot of vermilion paint mixed with blood from the comb of a brown chicken. Once this is done the dragon is "alive" and has to be treated with respect, presented with candles and incense, and protected from anything that might harm it.

HUNGRY GHOSTS

The Chinese believe that enormous numbers of ghosts roam the world. People may become ghosts if all their descendants die out, if they are murdered or commit suicide, or if they are unable to reach the afterworld because they did not have a proper funeral.

The seventh lunar month is considered by the Chinese to be especially dangerous because that is when the gates of hell open, allowing ghosts to roam wherever they like. Therefore it is necessary to placate wandering spirits by offering gifts of food and entertaining them with opera.

During the seventh month temporary wooden structures are built in open spaces. A stage is constructed for opera performances. There is also an altar where worshippers pray, while huge sticks of incense are burned night and day. Images of deities from the local temples are carried here in sedan chairs.

Believers also perform their own ceremonies during the month-long festival. Besides offering food, the people also burn paper clothing and spirit money to appease the hungry ghosts.

On the harbor decorated boats take offerings to ghosts who died at sea. While Buddhist monks or Daoist priests chant their liturgies on the boat, believers scatter rice upon the water and launch paper boats that are filled with gifts.

A girl carrying a lotus-shaped lantern during the Mid-Autumn Festival.

THE MID-AUTUMN FESTIVAL

The 15th day of the eighth lunar month is when the full moon shines brightest. This is also the time of the Mid-Autumn Festival. On this night children carry lanterns and look for Chang Er, the lady in the moon. According to legend Chang Er had a tyrannical husband who obtained

119

a potion that would make him immortal. Fearing for the well-being of her people, Chang Er drank the potion instead and flew to the moon.

Traditionally families would set up a table facing the moon and serve dishes with round foods such as apples, oranges, peaches, and mooncakes. Rice, wine, and tea are offered together with paper clothing and spirit money made of gold and silver paper. Shops sell special decorations and brightly colored lanterns. Today battery-operated plastic lanterns made in the shape of military tanks or Mickey Mouse are common.

Daoist priests perform Ta Chiu rituals to bless a village.

TA CHIU

In addition to lesser gods and ghosts Daoists believe in three great spirits—the Three Pure Ones. These pure spirits live in the stars, at the true source of life, and they are beyond the reach of change or decay.

The aim of Ta Chiu is to invite the Three Pure Ones down so that they will wipe away evil, restore peace and harmony, and renew life for entire village populations. Ordinary villagers leave the rituals to the Daoist priests. They are content to make offerings to their own patron gods, renounce evil, do good deeds, and feed the hungry ghosts.

The Ta Chiu ceremonies are carried out on several levels. Daoist priests perform a ceremony for the Three Pure Ones in the temple. Operas are staged, and offerings are brought to the patron deities, whose images have been brought out of the temple to a temporary shrine for the occasion. Birds and fishes are liberated as a symbolic life-giving gesture. Cleansing the altar, ritual bathing, fasting, and the disposal of items, which the priests collect and burn in a large paper boat, signifies purification.

Finally there are two spectacular closing ceremonies. The priests read the names of all the villagers from a huge list. After that they send the list to heaven by burning it on the back of a paper horse, before posting a red paper duplicate list on the wall for everyone to see. At midnight on the last day they preside over an enormous "clothes burning" session at which ghosts are fed, clothed, given money, and sent away. All the villagers eat a communal meal where the meat of the "golden pigs"—part of the offering to the gods—is looked upon as the most honored dish.

PUBLIC HOLIDAYS

Hong Kong has 17 public holidays. Among these are New Year's Day (January 1), Easter (March or April), Ching Ming (April), the Dragon Boat Festival (June), the Mid-Autumn Festival (September), and Christmas Day (December 25). Chinese New Year is a three-day public holiday in either January or February.

Some public holidays have changed since Hong Kong became a Special Administrative Region of China. Festivals according to the British calendar have been eliminated, and new festivals have been introduced. For example, the Queen's birthday, which used to be marked with two public holidays in June, is no longer celebrated. Liberation Day in August used to commemorate the Allied liberation of Hong Kong during World War II; it now commemorates the victory in the Second Sino-Japanese War. New holidays include June 1 and 2, which commemorate the change of sovereignty, and October 1 and 2, which celebrate China's National Day.

Christmas lightings in Hong Kong.

FOOD

HONG KONG'S SOPHISTICATED FOOD CULTURE reflects the richness of China's culinary arts. Chinese cuisine is probably one aspect of Chinese culture with which foreigners are most familiar. After all, Chinese restaurants can be found in almost every country. It is said that the Chinese are lucky people—wherever they travel, they can always eat their own cuisine! Much of the Chinese food available in Europe and North America is a variation of Cantonese cuisine, having been introduced by immigrants from Hong Kong.

A typical Hong Kong meal begins with tea. An appetizer, such as cold cuts of meat, follows. The main dishes follow next. There can be as many as 10 courses for a formal dinner such as a wedding banquet. For a more ordinary family meal there may be three or four dishes of meat and vegetables, plus a soup followed by dessert.

An old Chinese saying indicates how highly cuisine from Guangzhou (Canton) is regarded: "To be born in Suzhou, to live in Hangzhou, to eat in Guangzhou, and to die in Liuzhou."

Left: **Fresh vegetables are an important part of Cantonese cuisine.**

Opposite: **A diner sits in front of a roast meat store in Hong Kong.**

CANTONESE CUISINE

Because most Hong Kong Chinese originated in the area around Guangzhou (Canton), Cantonese cooking is by far the most popular cuisine in Hong Kong. This is what most people abroad know as Chinese food. Part of the reason for Cantonese cuisine's popularity is the way it is prepared. The food is light, cooked in a little water or oil, usually in a wok, and the process is quick. This seals in and preserves the flavors in the food.

Cantonese cuisine is known for its fresh, delicate flavors. Ingredients are prepared the same day and cooked just before serving. Seafood is so fresh, it hardly touches dry land before landing on the dinner table. In many seafood restaurants customers can actually choose the fish they wish to eat from tanks in which they are displayed. Chinese kitchens do not usually stock frozen and processed foods, although dried seafoods, such as shark's fin and abalone, are often used.

Many dishes, especially vegetables and fish, are steamed. This avoids overcooking and preserves the delicate flavors of the food. The use of hot and spicy sauces is not common in Cantonese cuisine. Sauces are used to enhance flavors, not overpower them. They usually contain ingredients with contrasting flavors, such as vinegar and sugar, or ginger and onion.

Barbecued meats—especially a type of sweet barbecued pork called *char siu* (chah syoo) and barbecued goose called *siu ngor* (syoo gnaw)— happen to be some Hong Kong favorites. Other popular Cantonese dishes include shark's fin soup, crabs steamed or cooked in black bean sauce, congee (thick Cantonese rice porridge), and the ubiquitous dim sum.

Food is cooked quickly in a wok at high heat.

Instead of saying "good morning" or "hello," many Chinese greet one another by asking if they have eaten.

124

DIM SUM

Dating from the 10th century, dim sum commands a special place in Cantonese cuisine. *Dim sum* literally means "to touch the heart." These bite-sized morsels of food are served in many Hong Kong restaurants, and their range is mind-boggling. You can choose from steamed or fried dumplings filled with meat or seafood, Chinese buns stuffed with sweet bean paste, spring rolls, chicken's feet, rice wrapped in leaves, and stuffed bean curd.

Dim sum forms part of the Chinese tradition of *yum cha* (Cantonese for "drinking tea"). It originated from the need to eat something during yum cha, when friends and colleagues would get together to discuss everything from business to family gossip. At a yum cha restaurant, the guests drink tea and choose dishes of dim sum from trays or bamboo baskets that are wheeled around.

There is an interesting tradition associated with yum cha. Instead of saying "thank you" when receiving tea, people sometimes tap the table twice with the knuckles of two fingers. Legend has it that a Chinese emperor traveled south disguised as an ordinary citizen, accompanied by his bodyguards. One day in a teahouse the emperor himself poured tea for one of his bodyguards. Instead of kneeling and bowing, which would have given away his emperor's identity, the bodyguard knocked on the table with two knuckles so that his fingers resembled kneeling legs. This gesture of respect gave rise to a tradition that is still practiced today.

YIN AND YANG FOOD

The Chinese believe that all food falls into three basic categories: Yang (or "heating") food warms the blood and reduces vital energy. Yin (or "cooling") food cools the blood and increases vital energy. Neutral food is balanced, and does not affect energy. Examples of yang food include fried items, lamb, mutton, chocolate, almonds, mangoes, and potato chips. Melons, apples, yogurt, pork, celery, salt, and bananas are all yin foods.

Winter is the time for yang food, because the blood needs to be heated, and summer is the time for yin food. When ordering food in restaurants the Hong Kong Chinese try to maintain a balance between yin and yang. Fried yang food may be teamed with steamed yin dishes, and "heating" meat dishes can be eaten along with some cooling vegetable dishes.

Fish and shellfish are traded at the fish market at Aberdeen.

DRINKS

Common nonalcoholic drinks in Hong Kong include soft drinks, many varieties of Chinese tea, and local specialties such as soya bean drinks. Fruit smoothies usually come with green or red beans, fruit pieces, and black grass jelly. Milk or ice cream is sometimes added.

Some Chinese drink Western wine, but it is more common to find local beer and spirits on the dining table. Chinese wine is often rice-based and distilled. Cognac is a popular drink, especially for entertaining favored guests. Like the exotic dishes served in restaurants, its cost is designed to impress. Brands such as Remy Martin and Courvoisier are consumed like water. Hong Kong is one of the world's biggest cognac consumers.

EXOTIC FOODS

The Cantonese are well known for what some consider their bizarre taste in meat. The Hong Kong Chinese are no exception. They believe that the more exotic the meat, the more salubrious, or wholesome, its effects on the health. Snake is boiled into a thick soup, as are shark's fins. Sea slugs, crocodiles, and sundry other creatures are prepared in a variety of ways. Frog's legs fried with ginger and scallions are thought to strengthen one's legs. Bird's nest soup is made from the dried mucus of the swift's salivary gland, which it uses to line its nest. Some Chinese delicacies, such as bear's paws, are banned in Hong Kong.

These rice wines contain baby rats and a snake. The Chinese believe they have curative powers.

TABLE ETIQUETTE

There is strict etiquette when eating with chopsticks. One must never use chopsticks to drum on the table, and it is most disrespectful to point them at another person or use them to gesture. When not in use chopsticks should be placed flat, not left standing vertically in a bowl, as the latter resembles incense offerings to the dead. Sometimes, for the sake of hygiene, diners will turn their chopsticks around and use the reverse end to take food from the serving dishes.

At mealtimes, whether at home or in a restaurant, it is customary to wait for everyone to be seated before beginning the meal. Children generally invite their elders to begin before helping themselves.

In Chinese meals, communal dishes are placed at the center of the table, and everyone helps themselves, making it a very sociable way to enjoy food.

Large Chinese dining tables in Hong Kong usually have a rotating platform in the center called a lazy susan, on which the serving dishes are placed. Diners help themselves to a morsel of the dish in front of them, and then rotate the lazy susan, sampling each dish along the way. Food should be taken from the top of the plate. It is considered rude to dig around for a morsel of food. The choice morsels should also be avoided. They should be offered to the elders at the table or to honored guests. A good host will always tend to his or her guests and urge them to eat their fill.

The Chinese do not pour soy sauce on their rice, because this would swamp the subtle flavors of the meal. Instead the sauce is placed in a small side dish.

Hong Kongers do not linger at the table. When the last course has been served and eaten, the meal is over.

TEA MYTHS AND LEGENDS

No one knows exactly when or how tea drinking started. Legends are filled with tales about the origins of tea. Some people believe that philosophers discovered tea, while others say that the beverage was first consumed as medicine.

One popular story about a pious monk says that the monk used to keep falling asleep while he was meditating. Frustrated with his "lazy eyelids," he took out a knife and cut his eyelids off. The monk threw his eyelids on the ground, where they developed roots and grew into the first tea plant, thus explaining why drinking tea helps one stay awake.

If you are uncertain which tea leaves are best, pay heed to Lu Yu's advice. The so-called Father of Tea wrote the *Tea Classic*, a three-volume tome dedicated to all topics related to tea. According to Lu Yu, the best tea leaves should have:

Creases like the leather boot of Tartar horsemen,
curl like the dewlap of a mighty bullock,
unfold like a mist rising out of a ravine,
gleam like a lake touched by a zephyr,
and be wet and soft like fine earth newly swept by rain.

CANTONESE STYLE EGG FOO YUNG

This recipe serves 3–4 people.

6 Chinese dried mushrooms,
    soaked for 30 minutes in hot water
2 oz (50 g) bean sprouts
6 water chestnuts (either fresh or
    canned), finely chopped
2 oz (50 g) spinach leaves, washed
4 tablespoons (60 ml) sunflower oil
2 oz (50 g) roast pork or *char siew*,
    cut into thin strips
4 eggs
$^1/_2$ teaspoon (2.5 ml) sugar
1 teaspoon (5 ml) rice wine or
    dry sherry
Salt and ground black pepper
Fresh coriander sprigs to garnish

Drain the mushrooms, cut and discard the stems, and then slice the caps finely and mix them with the vegetables. Heat half the oil in a large frying pan. Add the pork and vegetables. Toss the mixture over high heat for one minute, then set it aside.

Beat the eggs in a bowl. Add the partially cooked pork and vegetables and mix well. Wipe the frying pan clean and heat the remaining oil. Pour in the egg mixture and tilt the pan to cover the base. Once the omelet has set on the underside, sprinkle salt, pepper, and sugar on it. Invert a plate over the pan, and turn both over so that cooked side is now facing up on the plate. Slide the egg back into the pan to cook the other side. Drizzle with wine or sherry, garnish with coriander sprigs, and serve immediately.

FISH CONGEE

This recipe serves 2.

> $^{1}/_{2}$ cup long-grain rice
> 6 cups water
> 7 oz (200 g) raw fish fillets, thinly sliced
> $^{1}/_{2}$ teaspoon (2.5 ml) ginger, minced
> 2 sprigs spring onions, minced
> 1 tablespoon (15 ml) light soy sauce
> 2 teaspoons (5 ml) rice wine or dry sherry
> 1 tablespoon (15 ml) oil
> Pinch of salt or egg (optional)

Wash the rice thoroughly and place it in a deep pot with the water. Bring the water to a boil, then reduce to low heat and simmer for 1.5 to 2 hours. Stir occasionally to prevent the rice from sticking to the bottom, then let it stand for 15 minutes. As the rice mixture thickens, stir in the other ingredients and cook for one minute. Add a pinch of salt to taste, or whisk in a raw egg before serving.

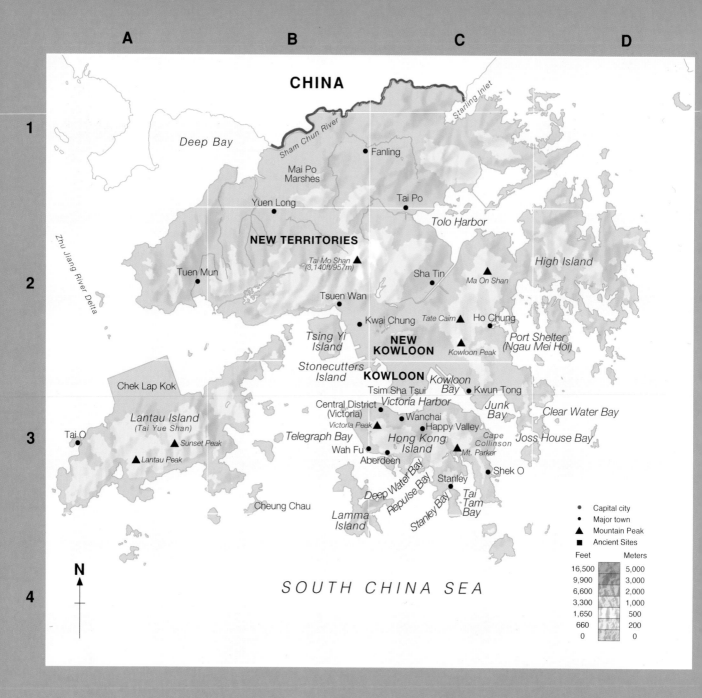

CHINA

Starling Inlet

Deep Bay

Sham Chun River

• Fanling

Mai Po
Marshes

Yuen Long •

• Tai Po

Tolo Harbor

NEW TERRITORIES

High Island

Tai Mo Shan ▲
(3,140ft/957m)

Sha Tin •

Ma On Shan ▲

Zhu Jiang River Delta

Tuen Mun •

Tsuen Wan •

Kwai Chung • *Tate Cairn* ▲ Ho Chung •

*Tsing Yi
Island*

**NEW
KOWLOON**

▲
Kowloon Peak

*Port Shelter
(Ngau Mei Hoi)*

*Stonecutters
Island*

KOWLOON

*Kowloon
Bay*

Tsim Sha Tsui • • Kwun Tong

Central District
(Victoria) • *Victoria Harbor*

*Junk
Bay*

Clear Water Bay

Chek Lap Kok

*Lantau Island
(Tai Yue Shan)*

▲ *Sunset Peak*

• Wanchai

Victoria Peak ▲ • Happy Valley

Tai O •

▲ *Lantau Peak*

Telegraph Bay

*Hong Kong
Island*

*Cape
Collinson*

Joss House Bay

Wah Fu •

• Aberdeen

▲
Mt. Parker

• Shek O

Stanley •

Deep Water Bay

Repulse Bay

*Tai
Tam
Bay*

Cheung Chau

*Lamma
Island*

Stanley Bay

• Capital city
• Major town
▲ Mountain Peak
■ Ancient Sites

Feet		Meters
16,500		5,000
9,900		3,000
6,600		2,000
3,300		1,000
1,650		500
660		200
0		0

SOUTH CHINA SEA

N

MAP OF HONG KONG

ECONOMIC HONG KONG

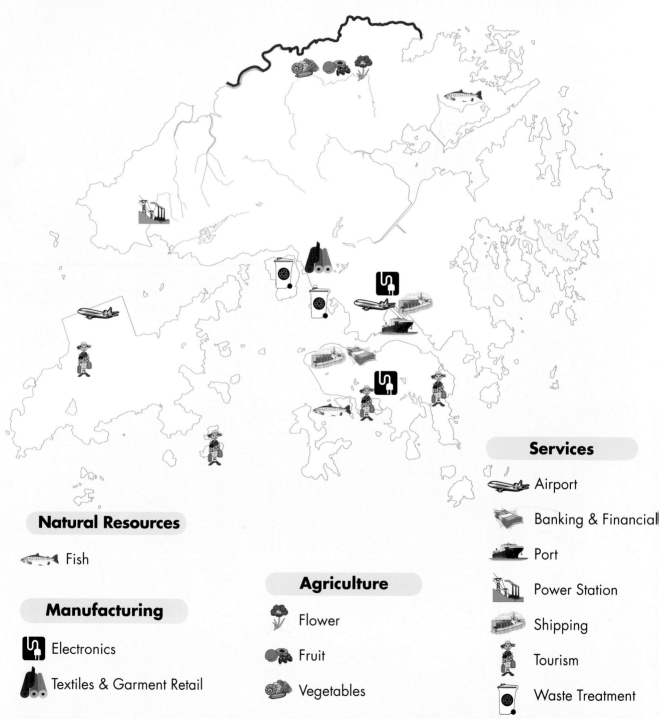

Natural Resources

Fish

Manufacturing

Electronics

Textiles & Garment Retail

Agriculture

Flower

Fruit

Vegetables

Services

Airport

Banking & Financial

Port

Power Station

Shipping

Tourism

Waste Treatment

ABOUT
THE ECONOMY

OVERVIEW
HONG KONG'S DEVELOPED ECONOMY is highly adaptable. In response to changing needs the territory shed its manufacturing past to morph into a high-value financial hub. Blessed with little more than a deep harbor and an industrious population, Hong Kong has worked hard to become what it is today—a sophisticated port, an internationally renowned trading center, and an economic force that continues to be the envy of many countries.

GROSS DOMESTIC PRODUCT (GDP)
$216.3 billion (2008 estimate)

GDP GROWTH
4.7 percent (2008 estimate)

INFLATION RATE
3.2 percent (2008 estimate)

LAND USE
Arable land 5 percent, country parks/protected areas 38 percent, others 57 percent (2005 estimates)

CURRENCY
HKD (Hong Kong dollar), 1 HKD = 100 cents
Coins: 10, 20, 50 cents
Notes: 10, 20, 50, 100, 500, 1,000 dollars
1 USD = 7.78 HKD (2008)

NATURAL RESOURCES
Port, feldspar

AGRICULTURAL PRODUCTS
Vegetables, poultry, pork, and fish

INDUSTRY
Banking and financial services, electronics, tourism, shipping, textiles and clothing, plastics

MAJOR EXPORTS
Machinery and electronics, textiles and apparel, footwear, plastics, printed materials

MAJOR IMPORTS
Consumer goods, foodstuffs, raw materials, and semi-manufactured goods

MAIN TRADE PARTNERS
China, Japan, United States, Taiwan, Singapore (2006)

WORKFORCE
3.64 million: Retail and services 44 percent, finance 20 percent, manufacturing 7.5 percent, communications 7 percent (2008 estimate)

UNEMPLOYMENT RATE
4.0 percent (2008 estimate)

FOREIGN RESERVES
$ 132 billion (2008 estimate)

CULTURAL HONG KONG

Mai Po Marshes
This nature reserve is home to more than 300 different species of birds, including the endangered imperial eagle. Leopard cats and otters have also been sighted.

Man Mo Temple
One of Hong Kong's oldest and most famous landmarks dedicated to two deities: Man Cheung, the god of literature; and Kwan Ti, the red-cheeked god of war. Interestingly, the latter is the patron saint of the police force and triad societies, both traditional archenemies.

Temple Street
A bargain hunter's dream come true this nightly market is crammed with stalls that sell clothes, silk items, and assorted bric-a-brac.

Star Ferry Service
Hop onboard for a 10-minute ride between Kowloon and Hong Kong Island and take in some truly awesome city sights.

Central Market
Pop by early in the morning for an authentic "wet" (fresh food) market experience. Spread over four levels, the cacophony of sights, sounds, and smells is not for the fainthearted.

Cheung Chau Island
The famed Bun Festival is unique to Hong Kong. Following three to four days of Daoist religious observances, contestants used to race to climb huge scaffolds festooned with buns symbolizing good luck.

Victoria Harbor/Victoria Peak
Be mesmerized by "A Symphony of Lights." Tsim Sha Tsui provides great waterfront views for the nightly displays. Or jump onto the Peak tram for a bird's-eye view of Hong Kong's spectacular night scenery.

Buddha at Po Lin (Precious Lotus) Monastery
Visitors to Po Lin can climb 268 steps to see Asia's largest seated Buddha statue, the Po Lin Buddha. This uphill trek offers panoramic views of the South China Sea and surrounding islands.

Disneyland Resort
Asia's second Disneyland offers fun for the entire family, with hair-raising rides, fairy-tale castles, and familiar cartoon characters.

Ocean Park Hong Kong
Have a whale of a time at this all-in-one entertainment facility. Attractions include stomach-churning rides, aquariums, aviaries, animal shows, and a Dolphin University for both the young and the young at heart.

ABOUT
THE CULTURE

OFFICIAL NAME
Hong Kong Special Administrative Region (SAR) of China

FLAG DESCRIPTION
Red with a white five-petal bauhinia flower in the center

INDEPENDENCE
None (Handed over to China on July 1, 1997)

MAJOR URBAN AREAS
Central, Kowloon, Wan Chai

POPULATION
7.03 million (2008 estimate)

BIRTHRATE
7.34 births per 1,000 (2007 estimate)

DEATH RATE
6.45 deaths per 1,000 (2007 estimate)

LIFE EXPECTANCY
81.7 years (2007 estimate)

POPULATION GROWTH RATE
0.6 percent (2007 estimate)

ETHNIC GROUPS
Chinese 95 percent, Filipino 1.6 percent, others 3.4 percent (2006 estimate)

RELIGIOUS GROUPS
Buddhist and Daoist 90 percent, Christian 10 percent (2007 estimate)

MAIN LANGUAGES
Chinese (Cantonese) 91.7 percent (official), other Chinese dialects 4.4 percent, English 2.8 percent (official), others 1.1 percent (2006 estimate)

LITERACY RATE
93.5 percent (2007 estimate)

IMPORTANT HOLIDAYS
New Year (January 1); Chinese New Year (late January or early February); Good Friday and Easter Monday (March/April); Ching Ming Festival (April); Buddha's Birthday/Vesak Day (April/May); Labor Day (May 1); Dragon Boat Festival (May/June); Hong Kong SAR Establishment Day (July 1); Sino-Japanese War Victory Day (August); Mid-Autumn Festival (late September or early October); National Day (October 1 and 2); Christmas (December 25)

TIME LINE

IN HONG KONG	IN THE WORLD

4000 B.C.
Early settlers inhabit the area around Hong Kong.

200 B.C.
Unification of Chinese empire; Hong Kong Island is ruled by a governor based in China's Canton province.

A.D. 1685
British and French merchants start trading tea and silk with Hong Kong.

1842
China defeated in First Opium War; Hong Kong Island is ceded to the British.

1861
China concedes Kowloon Peninsula to Great Britain.

1889
China signs treaty leasing the New Territories to Britain for 99 years.

1941
British forces surrender, leading to Japanese occupation of Hong Kong.

1945
Hong Kong reverts to British colonial rule following Japanese defeat at the end of World War II.

1949
Communist Party gains victory in China; refugees flock to Hong Kong.

1950–53
United States imposes sanctions on China during the Korean War; Hong Kong develops its own manufacturing base.

1967
Hong Kong rocked by political riots arising from the Chinese Cultural Revolution.

753 B.C.
Rome is founded.

A.D. 600
Height of Mayan civilization

1776
U.S. Declaration of Independence

1789–99
The French Revolution

1861
The U.S. Civil War begins.

1869
The Suez Canal is opened.

1914
World War I begins.

1945
The United States drops atomic bombs on Hiroshima and Nagasaki.

1949
The North Atlantic Treaty Organization (NATO) is formed.

1957
The Russians launch Sputnik.

1966–69
The Chinese Cultural Revolution

IN HONG KONG	IN THE WORLD
1975 Indochina War leads to influx of 100,000 Vietnamese refugees to the colony.	
1982 Then–British Prime Minister Margaret Thatcher visits Beijing to discuss Hong Kong's future.	
1984 Sino-British Joint Declaration states that Hong Kong will return to Chinese rule in 1997.	
	1986 Nuclear disaster at Chernobyl in Ukraine
1988 Beijing publishes Basic Law guaranteeing the rights of Hong Kong citizens.	
1989 More than one million Hong Kongers protest the Tiananmen Square massacre, amid increasing fears about their return to Chinese sovereignty.	
	1991 Breakup of the Soviet Union
1996 Hong Kong wins its first Olympic gold medal.	
1997 Hong Kong becomes a Special Administrative Region (SAR) of China.	**1997** Hong Kong is returned to China.
1998 Asian financial crises cause Hong Kong's stock markets to tumble.	
	2001 Terrorists crash planes in New York, Washington, D.C., and Pennsylvania.
2003 Severe acute respiratory syndrome (SARS) epidemic brings Hong Kong to a standstill.	**2003** War in Iraq begins.
2007 Hong Kong celebrates the first decade after its handover to China.	

GLOSSARY

char siu
Sweet barbecued pork.

chi
Spirit, energy.

congee
The English name for Cantonese rice porridge ("juk" in Cantonese).

dao (*dow*, **rhymes with** *now*)
In the Daoist religion, the spiritual path that leads to immortality.

dim sum
Dumplings or other foods eaten in small portions, particularly while drinking tea.

feng shui (fung soy)
An ancient system of attaining good health and fortune through a harmonious environment.

gweilo (gwy-loh)
Caucasian person (literally "foreign devil").

laisee (ly-see)
Red packets of lucky money given at Chinese New Year and other special occasions.

laissez-faire
The practice of noninterference in the affairs of others; often used to describe a government with minimal involvement in economic affairs.

joss stick
Incense stick; *joss* means "luck."

juk
Cantonese name for porridge.

junk
A Chinese sailing ship.

karaoke
Singing along to prerecorded instrumental music.

mah-jongg
A Chinese game of tiles played by four people.

mooncakes
Pastries filled with sweet lotus paste.

siu ngor (syoo gnaw)
Barbecued goose.

spirit money
Pretend paper money that is burned as an offering to gods or ancestral ghosts.

tai chi
A Chinese martial art characterized by meditative exercises.

weiqi (way-chee)
A Chinese board game.

yang
Energy that is positive and active.

yin
Energy that is negative and passive.

yum cha
To drink tea.

zham cha (tsum chah)
To serve tea.

FURTHER INFORMATION

BOOKS

Fallon, Steve. *Lonely Planet Hong Kong Encounter*. Victoria, Australia: Lonely Planet Publications, 2007.

Morris, Jan. *Hong Kong*. New York: Vintage Books, 1997.

O'Reilly, James, Larry Habegger, and Sean O'Reilly. *Travellers' Tales Hong Kong*. Redwood City, CA: Travelers' Tales Ltd., 1998.

Roberti, Mark. *The Fall of Hong Kong: China's Triumph and Britain's Betrayal*. Toronto, Canada: John Wiley & Sons, 1996.

Wright, Rachel. *Living and Working in Hong Kong: The Complete Practical Guide to Expatriate Life in China's Gateway*. Oxford, U.K.: How To Books Ltd., 2007.

WEB SITES

E-Journal on Hong Kong Cultural and Social Studies. www.hku.hk/hkcsp/ccex/ehkcss01/index.htm

Environmental Concerns. www.epd.gov.hk and www.friendsoftheharbour.org

Hong Kong Tourist Board. www.discoverhongkong.com

News and current affairs in Hong Kong. www.scmp.com.hk

Restaurant and shopping information. www.bcmagazine.net

FILMS

Chungking Express. Jet Tone Productions, 1994.

Fists of Fury. Golden Harvest, 1972.

In the Mood for Love. Paradis Films, 2001.

Rush Hour 2. Hiett Designs/New Line Cinema, 2001.

BIBLIOGRAPHY

Information Services Department. *Hong Kong Special Administrative Region, The First Five Years 1997–2002.* Hong Kong: Information Services Department, 2002.

Ma, Ngok. *Political Development in Hong Kong: State, Political Society and Civil Society.* Hong Kong: Hong Kong University Press, 2007.

Miller, Donald, and De Roo, Gert (editors). *Urban Environmental Planning.* Hampshire, England: Avebury, 1997.

Morris, Sallie, and Hsiung, Deh-ta. *Taste of Asia.* London: Anness Publishing Limited, 2005.

Sterling, Richard, and Elizabeth Chong (coauthors and editors). *World Food Hong Kong.* Victoria, Australia: Lonely Planet Publications, 2001.

Thomas, Ted, and Nicole Turner. *What's Going to Happen in 1997 in Hong Kong?* Singapore: Simon & Schuster (Asia), 1996.

Vickers, Clare. *Culture Smart! Hong Kong.* London, England: Kuperad, 2005.

Wei, Betty, and Elizabeth Li. *Culture Shock! Hong Kong.* Portland, OR: Graphic Arts Center, 1995.

Wong, Kwan-Yiu, and Shen, Jianfa (editors). *Resource Management, Urbanization and Governance in Hong Kong and the Zhujiang Delta.* Hong Kong: The Chinese University Press, 2002.

Wong, Yiu-Ching (editor). "One Country, Two Systems" in *Crisis: Hong Kong's Transformation Since the Handover.* Lanham, MD: Lexington Books, 2004.

Yahuda, Michael. *Hong Kong: China's Challenge.* New York: Routledge, 1996.

Central Intelligence Agency World Factbook (select Hong Kong from country list). www.cia.gov/cia/publications/factbook/index.html

Hong Kong Government's Information Services Department. www.info.gov.hk

Mongabay—Overview of Environment. www.mongabay.com

MSN Encarta—General Information.www.encarta.msn.com

INDEX